The Wife of Bath's Prologue and Tale

by Geoffrey Chaucer

Richard Swan

Series Editors:
Nicola Onyett and Luke McBratney

HODDER
EDUCATION
AN HACHETTE UK COMPANY

The publisher would like to thank the following for permission to reproduce copyright material:

Acknowledgments:

Geoffrey Chaucer: from *The Wife of Bath's Prologue* and *Tale* (1478); **pp.20, 22, 74: James Winny:** from Introduction *to The Wife of Bath's Tale* (Cambridge University Press, 1965)

Photo credits:

p.1 © The Granger Collection / TopFoto; **p.7** © Granger, NYC. / Alamy Stock Photo; **p.10** © HIP / TopFoto; **p.11** © Lebrecht Music and Arts Photo Library / Alamy Stock Photo; **p.21** © Courtesy Everett Collection / REX / Shutterstock; **p.31** Reproduced by the kind permission of the Syndics of Cambridge University Library; **p.32** © Nigel Norrington / ArenaPAL / TopFoto; **p.38** © World History Archive / Topfoto; **p.43** © Mary Evans Picture Library / Alamy Stock Photo; **p.49** © Georgios Kollidas / 123RF.com; **p.57** © Photos 12 / Alamy Stock Photo

Orders: please contact Bookpoint Ltd, 130 Milton Park, Abingdon, Oxon OX14 4SB. Telephone: (44) 01235 827720. Fax: (44) 01235 400454. Lines are open 9.00–17.00, Monday to Saturday, with a 24-hour message answering service. Visit our website at www.hoddereducation.co.uk

© Richard Swan, 2016

First published in 2016 by

Hodder Education

An Hachette UK Company,

Carmelite House, 50 Victoria Embankment

London EC4Y 0DZ

Impression number	5	4	3	2	1
Year		2020	2019	2018	2017	2016

Cover photo (and throughout) © Grape_vein/iStockphoto/ Thinkstock/Getty Images

Illustrations by Philip Allen

Typeset in 11/13pt Bliss Light by Integra Software Services Pvt. Ltd., Pondicherry, India

Printed in Italy

A catalogue record for this title is available from the British Library.

ISBN 978-1-4718-5419-4

Contents

Using this guide

Why read this guide?

The purposes of this A-level Literature Guide are to enable you to organise your thoughts and responses to the text, to deepen your understanding of key features and aspects, and to help you address the particular requirements of examination questions and non-exam assessment (NEA) tasks in order to obtain the best possible grade. This guide will also prove useful to those of you writing an NEA piece on the text, as it provides a number of summaries, lists, analyses and references to help with the content and construction of the assignment.

Note that teachers and examiners are seeking above all else evidence of an *informed personal response to the text*. A guide such as this can help you to understand the text and form your own opinions, and it can suggest areas to think about – but it cannot replace your own ideas and responses as an informed and autonomous reader.

How to make the most of this guide

You may find it useful to read sections of this guide when you need them, rather than reading it through from start to finish. For example, you may find it helpful to read the 'Contexts' section before you start reading the text, or to read the 'Summaries and commentaries' section in conjunction with the text – whether to back up your first reading of it at school or college or to help you revise. The sections relating to the Assessment Objectives will be especially useful in the weeks leading up to the exam.

Key elements

This guide is designed to help you raise your achievement in your examination response to *The Wife of Bath's Prologue* and *Tale*. It is intended for you to use throughout your AS/A-level English literature course. It will help you when you are studying the play for the first time and also during your revision.

The following features have been used throughout this guide to help you focus your understanding of the play:

Context

Context boxes give contextual evidence that relates directly to particular aspects of the text.

Build critical skills

Broaden your thinking about the text by answering the questions in the **Build critical skills** boxes. These help you to consider your own opinions in order to develop your skills of criticism and analysis.

Taking it further ▶

Taking it further boxes suggest and provide further background or illuminating parallels to the text.

CRITICAL VIEW

Critical view boxes highlight a particular critical viewpoint that is relevant to an aspect of the main text. This allows you to develop the higher-level skills needed to come up with your own interpretation of a text.

TASK

Tasks are short and focused. They allow you to engage directly with a particular aspect of the text.

Top ten quotation ◁ Top ten quotation

A cross-reference to **Top ten quotations** (see p.93 of this guide), where each quotation is accompanied by a commentary that shows why it is important.

Introduction

The Wife of Bath's Prologue and *Tale* forms part of *The Canterbury Tales*, the much longer work that provides its immediate context. *The Canterbury Tales* is a medieval story collection; it was written by Geoffrey Chaucer towards the end of the fourteenth century and set in the framework of a pilgrimage from London to Canterbury. Chaucer introduces some 30 pilgrims, who then tell stories in order to pass the time as they travel on horseback towards their destination. This device allows Chaucer to create a wide variety of narrative voices and to include a very diverse collection of stories, ranging from the bawdy ribaldry of *The Miller's Tale* to the romantic and serious story of courtly love in *The Knight's Tale*. Most of the tales are in verse but two are in prose; one of these is *The Parson's Tale*, which is not a story at all but rather a lengthy sermon on the subject of the seven deadly sins.

The Wife of Bath's Prologue and *Tale* is presented by a character called Alison, a widow from Bath, who is able to travel independently on the pilgrimage because of her wealth, derived partly from her five marriages and partly from her trade of cloth-making. Already this marks her out as a highly unusual figure in the Middle Ages, a period when women were mostly subservient to their husbands and were rarely able to travel alone, and whose voices would not normally be heard. Yet this is only the beginning of what makes *The Wife of Bath's Prologue* and *Tale* such a rewarding text to study.

The character of the narrator herself is the central point of interest. Alison is a 'larger than life' figure, extravagantly dressed, forthright and uninhibited. Her main topic is marriage, and she regales her listeners with a sometimes bawdy account of her own sexuality and her experiences with her five husbands. You need to understand this aspect of the text fully, and to decide for yourself whether Chaucer is providing a naturalistic portrait of a sexually liberated woman or whether he is providing a satirical representation of Lust, one of the seven deadly sins. To do this you need to compare the contexts of the tale's production in the fourteenth century and its reception in the twenty-first. Our contemporary world has very different values and beliefs, particularly about the place and status of women in society.

The Wife of Bath's Prologue and *Tale* is also unusual in that its prologue, where the Wife describes her life and marriages, is twice as long as the tale that she then tells (about a knight who rapes a maiden and must seek redemption for his crime against women). This seeming imbalance is important and will be another major feature of your studies. In a way the text is like a binary star: the larger prologue and the shorter tale revolve around each other, linked by theme and purpose.

Finally, the whole of *The Canterbury Tales* is meant to entertain, and the comedy and high spirits of *The Wife of Bath's Prologue* and *Tale* need to be borne firmly in mind even when you are considering the underlying seriousness of the issues raised.

Synopsis

The Wife of Bath, whose name is Alison, is one of the 30 characters that Chaucer assembles at the Tabard Inn in Southwark, all going on a pilgrimage to the shrine of Thomas Becket at Canterbury. They agree to tell stories on the way to pass the time. Chaucer never completed the scheme, so we do not know what would have preceded the Wife of Bath's contribution, but her tale is succeeded by those of the Friar and the Summoner.

The Wife of Bath begins by introducing her theme, which is marriage and the relative power of the man and the woman within the relationship. Whether by accident or design her prologue extends itself to 850 lines of verse, more than twice the length of the tale that follows it.

Because *The Wife of Bath's Prologue* and *Tale* has no link to a preceding tale, the Wife's opening statement is strikingly emphatic. She claims that her own experience is more than sufficient for her to speak of the 'wo that is in marriage' (line 3) because she has been married five times (and is now a widow). She claims that she therefore does not need to cite authorities such as the Bible to justify her opinions, although this would have been the normal procedure for a medieval person trying to argue a case.

There are immediate ironies in her apparently simple opening. Her prologue and tale are full of references to the kind of authorities she claims she does not need, and it is far from clear whether she or her husbands have suffered most from the woes of marriage.

Her long prologue is mainly an account of her own experiences during her marriages, after an opening section in which she reveals and defends her views of marriage. She starts by justifying her five marriages, which are not illegal but which seem to contravene the view that a Christian should marry only once. She is not suited to chastity, she claims, and therefore will always choose to marry and lead a full sexual life.

The Pardoner interrupts her discourse, claiming that he had been about to get married but that she has frightened him off. She brushes him aside and proceeds to tell the audience about her marriages. She lumps her first three husbands together, saying that they were 'goode' (line 196) because they were rich and old, but they were sexually inadequate and she takes delight in explaining how she talked to them and fooled them.

Her fourth husband is briefly described. He was a 'badde' husband, partly because he had a mistress, but mainly because he was not under her control. She revenges herself by making him jealous, and when he dies she is dismissive about him.

▲ The Wife of Bath, in an image taken from the Ellesmere manuscript of *The Canterbury Tales* (c.1410)

Context

The character of the Wife of Bath was a great rarity in medieval times, being a woman of independent means. By judicious marriages, and by convenient widowhood, the Wife has been able to amass a considerable fortune, which has enabled her to travel and act independently. It is worth reflecting that the only other women on the pilgrimage are nuns, who would be undertaking the journey for spiritual reasons. Everybody else is male.

The remainder of her prologue is reserved for an account of her marriage to her fifth husband, Jankin. She married him for love, but he turned out to be a misogynist and took pleasure in reading to her from a book of anti-feminist writings. The Wife gives copious examples of this material, in order to show why she became progressively exasperated. In the end she could bear it no longer, and ripped three leaves out of his precious book and hit him. He retaliated, but was instantly remorseful. This allowed the Wife to gain complete control over him. She forced him to burn his book, and says they thereafter lived happily.

The Friar comments, not untruthfully, that this is 'a long preamble of a tale' (line 831), provoking an altercation with the Summoner. This will serve as grounds for the tales that each later tells at the other's expense, but here it merely marks the transition to the Wife of Bath's tale.

After her first-hand account of the woes of marriage, the Wife turns to the form of a fairy tale for the story that she tells to the pilgrims. The theme, however, is the same – the relationship between men and women, and the issue of who will be dominant in a relationship.

The tale is set in the days of King Arthur and features one of Arthur's knights, who contravenes all knightly codes and honour by raping a young woman. As a punishment he is set the task of discovering 'what thing is it that wommen moost desiren' (line 905). He travels around and eventually encounters a mysterious old hag who promises to assist him, but only if he promises to fulfil her next demand. The answer she reveals to him is that women most desire sovereignty, that is, dominance over men. The hag's demand is that the knight marries her. He reluctantly does so, but is so ill-behaved on their wedding night that she lectures him about polite behaviour. He then places himself wholly in her power, whereupon she is magically transformed into a beautiful woman and they live happily together.

Summaries and commentaries

Target your thinking

- How can you build your critical vocabulary to include a wide range of terms that are useful for the study of Chaucer? (**AO1**)
- By what methods does Chaucer entertain his audience and bring the Wife to life? (**AO2**)
- In what ways will your developing understanding of the Bible and medieval interpretations of it help you respond to Chaucer's text? (**AO3**)

The Wife of Bath's Prologue

The Wife of Bath's contribution to *The Canterbury Tales* is unique, because her prologue to her tale is twice as long as the tale itself. The Pardoner is the only other pilgrim with a significant personal prologue, and that is only 130 lines followed by a tale of 500 lines. The Wife's vastly extended prologue means that it is a major focus of study for students, but it can be daunting because it seems rambling and unwieldy.

Chaucer presents the Wife's discussion of marriage in three major components. First, she sets out her theoretical arguments about marriage, its nature and purpose, and particularly the issue of multiple (serial) marriages (lines 1–162 of her prologue); second, she relates her practical experience (lines 194–828), and finally she gives an *exemplum* (formal example) in the form of her tale. Overall, *The Wife of Bath's Prologue* and *Tale* is part of a much more extended exploration of the nature of marriage in *The Canterbury Tales* (see the 'Contexts' section on the 'marriage group' of tales, on p.65 of this guide).

Lines 1–3

The Wife claims that, even if there were no textual authorities, her own experience is sufficient to justify her speaking about the woes of marriage.

Commentary: The opening of *The Wife of Bath's Prologue* is the key to understanding the whole text. Her use of the word 'experience' is a direct challenge to the traditional and male-dominated authority of the medieval Church. She asserts the validity of her own experience and judgement, and in this way she can seem thoroughly modern. This issue is so important that it is treated separately in the 'Themes' section on page 20 of this guide. You must ultimately make up your own mind whether the Wife is to be admired or condemned for her self-reliance.

TASK

Read the section on biblical exegesis carefully and then decide for yourself how expert the Wife is at interpreting her quoted sources. What conclusions about her character do you draw?

Lines 4–61

The Wife uses biblical examples to defend her right to marry more than once. The medieval Catholic Church taught that virginity was the most blessed state. Monogamous marriage was also good, but widows were discouraged from re-marrying. The Wife therefore feels that her five marriages, although sequential, need some justification.

Commentary: There is an immediate irony in the fact that the Wife opens her prologue by stating the fact that she does not need 'auctoritees', and then goes on to use them at length in this section. The implication she clearly intends to give is that, although her argument does not require them, these authorities in fact support her case.

Exegesis is interpretation of or commentary on a text, particularly the Bible and similar authorities. Such commentary was a common and vital part of all medieval scholarship. The Wife of Bath uses exegesis as an important part of her argument, and so it is necessary to examine how she uses her authorities in order to support her case.

For each of the following examples, look at the biblical source that the Wife refers to as well as at the relevant lines in her prologue. You should then explore as many other examples as you can; your edition will give you the necessary information about sources.

The modern student is at a considerable disadvantage here, because the Bible is no longer a familiar text. Chaucer's audience would have known all the Bible stories extremely well, whereas we have to work our way through the detail.

The first example is from *The Wife of Bath's Prologue*, lines 21–22:

> ...why that the fifthe man
> Was noon housbonde to the Samaritan?

This refers to a passage from John's Gospel, Chapter 4, verses 16–18:

> *Jesus said to her, 'Go, call your husband, and come here.'*
> *The woman answered him, 'I have no husband.' Jesus said to her, 'You are right in saying, "I have no husband"; for thou have had five husbands, and he whom you now have is not your husband; this you said truly.'*

The wife is trying to justify the concept of multiple marriages, but she seems to have simply misread this passage. The Bible clearly says that the Samaritan woman has had five husbands in the past, and is now living with someone to whom she is not married.

The second example is from the prologue, lines 28–29:

> God bad us for to wexe and multiplie;
> That gentil text kan I wel understonde.

Genesis, Chapter 1, verse 22 says:

Be fruitful, and multiply.

The irony is contained in line 29. It is true that God in Genesis commanded mankind to be fruitful and multiply, and the Wife uses this as a justification for her obsession with sex. But the Catholic Church, in keeping with Genesis, taught that the only reason for sexual intercourse was procreation – which the Wife of Bath seems to have no interest in. She never mentions having children (how did she avoid them?), and later tells us that she married her husbands for their wealth and for sexual pleasure. In this sense she seems to have completely failed to understand the significance of the Bible passage that she quotes. This same failure occurs later in her prologue (lines 113–16):

> I wol bistowe the flour of al myn age
> In the actes and in fruit of mariage.
> Telle me also, to what conclusion
> Were membres maad of generacion…?

The third example of exegesis comes from the prologue, lines 35–38:

> Lo, heere, the wise king, daun Salomon;
> I trowe he hadde wives more than oon.
> As wolde God it were leveful unto me
> To be refreshed half so ofte as he!

1 Kings, Chapter 11, verses 3–4 says:

He had seven hundred wives, princesses, and three hundred concubines; and his wives turned away his heart. For when Solomon was old his wives turned away his heart after other gods; and his heart was not wholly true to the Lord his God.

The Wife refers to Solomon because he is traditionally known for being wise – 'the Wisdom of Solomon' – and by implication what is right for him must be right for anybody. But Chaucer's audience would have been instantly alive to the implications of her reference. There are two issues here. The first is the outrageous desire of the Wife to be 'refreshed' – itself an interesting euphemism – half as often as a man who has a thousand sexual partners. Even a modern audience might baulk at a woman who openly expressed such nymphomaniac tendencies. Second, Solomon's profusion of wives causes him to turn his heart away from God – and this is the example the Wife says she wishes to follow. She therefore ironically condemns her own behaviour twice over with this single biblical reference. Indeed, she goes further, because in her next line she says, 'Which yifte of God hadde he for alle his wives!' (line 39). Presumably she is envying Solomon for the fact that God has permitted him all these wives (and the attendant 'refreshing'). In fact, Solomon's reward for his behaviour, which led to him turning away from God, was that God said he would

> **Build critical skills**
>
> How does the use of rhyming couplets add to the impact of what the Wife is saying?

deprive Solomon's sons of the kingdom. Chaucer's audience would know that Solomon's behaviour led to punishment rather than praise.

It is clear from these examples that the Wife of Bath is a most unreliable interpreter of the Bible. She is highly selective about the aspects that she chooses to emphasise, and even here she seems to misunderstand or misread what the Bible is saying. This is an important issue for the modern reader, who must laboriously reconstruct what would have been plain and obvious to a medieval audience.

There is a definite gap between the Wife's apparently limited understanding and the breadth of reference and erudition shown throughout *The Wife of Bath's Prologue* and *Tale*. This is simply explained because the sophisticated learning belongs to Chaucer, who uses it for his own purposes. He assigns this knowledge to the Wife so that she is enabled to create her case.

Lines 62–114

Taking it further ▷

Investigate the types of education available to women in the Middle Ages. How might the Wife of Bath have come by her knowledge of the Bible and her ability to interpret it? Remember that the Bible would normally be available only in Latin; it was only in Chaucer's lifetime that Wycliffe began producing a translation into English, which was condemned by the Church.

The Wife explains that although virginity is the ideal, she is not suited to it. She will therefore always choose to marry.

Commentary: She continues to use the Bible for her defence, referring to 1 Corinthians, Chapter 7 and stating that, although St Paul recommended virginity, he did not insist on it. She explains that she is not such a perfect person: 'Of myn estaat I nil nat make no boost' (line 98). She continues with her biblical exegesis:

> For wel ye knowe, a lord in his houshold,
> He nath nat every vessel al of gold;
> Somme been of tree, and doon hir lord servise.
>
> (lines 99–101)

This refers to 2 Timothy, Chapter 2, verses 20–22:

> *In a great house there are not only vessels of gold and of silver but also of wood and earthenware, and some for noble use, and some for ignoble. If anyone purifies himself from what is ignoble, then he will be a vessel for noble use, consecrated and useful to the master of the house, ready for any good work. So shun youthful passions and aim at righteousness, faith, love, and peace, along with those who call upon the Lord from a pure heart.*

The Wife's argument seems superficially reasonable. She and the Bible agree that not every household utensil is made of gold. But she uses this as an argument for saying that wooden vessels are equally useful, and therefore equally worthy. There is an apparent humility in her acceptance that she is not gold, but is willing to serve as humble wood. The Bible passage, however, clearly has a different message. It says that wooden vessels are ignoble, and that every person should attempt to purify themselves so that they are noble – metaphorically, every person can and should become a golden vessel fit for the Lord's service. The Bible specifically states that people should shun 'youthful passions', but these seem to be what the Wife claims is her special gift. Her interpretation is therefore totally at odds with the biblical original.

Lines 115–62

She argues that the sexual organs are there for use, and that she will therefore use hers 'As frely as my Makere hath it sent' (line 150). She claims that she dominated her husbands.

Commentary: She is on dangerous ground with this argument, as the medieval Church condemned sexual intercourse for pleasure. Its function was for 'ese / of engendrure' (lines 127–28), i.e. to provide children, but the Wife never mentions having any. Moreover, rather than use sex for its proper purpose, she says that she uses it as a means to dominate her husbands. There is comedy in her assertion that her husband 'shal it have bothe eve and morwe' (line 152), because it sounds more like a punishment than a delight. She promises 'tribulacion withal / Upon his flessh' (lines 156–57), because she has 'power duringe al my lyf / Upon his propre body, and noght he' (lines 158–59). As usual, she completely ignores the reciprocal nature of the marriage bond, stated in 1 Corinthians, Chapter 7, verses 4–5: 'The wife cannot claim her body as her own; it is her husband's. Equally, the husband cannot claim his body as his own; it is his wife's.' She ignores the sentences that she does not like and claims dominance.

Lines 163–93: The Pardoner's interruption

The Pardoner interrupts the Wife's monologue, claiming that he had been about to get married but that she has put him off the idea completely.

Commentary: Chaucer adds to the verisimilitude of *The Canterbury Tales* by having the Pardoner interrupt the Wife, apparently appalled by her. She rapidly puts him in his place and continues. There is a dramatic irony here for Chaucer's audience; the Pardoner himself is a supremely gifted and fluent speaker, and it is amusing to see him silenced so quickly by a woman who can outtalk even him. There is a further irony in that the Pardoner has been identified in *The General Prologue* as a probable eunuch, with a suggestion that he is in a homosexual relationship with the Summoner. Chaucer's audience would have laughed both at the dismay caused by the Wife's remarks and at the comic unsuitability of the pilgrim who voices that dismay with an absurd claim of impending marriage. The interruption also has a structural purpose in demarcating the transition from the Wife's theoretical introduction to her relation of practical experience with her five husbands.

Taking it further ▶

Research the different attitudes to sex in the fourteenth and the twenty-first centuries. Do not be simplistic about this, however; many modern people still have particular attitudes about what is and is not morally appropriate, while the medieval Wife of Bath seems to have a liberated attitude.

▲ An image of the Pardoner from a fifteenth-century manuscript

TASK

Study the portraits of the Pardoner, the Friar and the Summoner in *The General Prologue*. Why do you think Chaucer chose these characters to comment on the Wife of Bath's discourse?

Build critical skills

Look at the remarks made by the Pardoner and those of the Friar and Summoner at the end of the prologue (lines 829–56). How do their reactions to the Wife's prologue influence your own?

Top ten quotation

TASK

Examine carefully the way that Chaucer varies the treatment of the husbands. To deal with all five individually would be tedious, so he groups the first three together, treats the fourth briefly, and then focuses on the fifth. What comments can you make about his narrative method here?

Lines 194–451: Her first three husbands

The Wife declares that three of her husbands 'were goode, and two were badde' (line 196). She will deal with the latter two individually, but the first three are lumped together and dealt with as if they are indistinguishable. She explains at length the way she talked to them and her means of countering their objections to her behaviour.

Commentary: The Wife's claim that her first three husbands were 'goode men' is immediately qualified by the addition that they were 'riche, and olde' (line 197); it is in this that their 'goodness' lay as far as the Wife is concerned. Their age and feebleness enabled her to dominate them and turn their own arguments against them. An added advantage is that they each soon died, so that she was able to move on to another (rich) man.

In this section the Wife marshals much of the current anti-feminist opinion of the time. The Wife refutes it, but in doing so seems to exemplify much of what she cites. This crucial aspect of the text is dealt with in the 'Themes' section, on page 22 of this guide.

It is worth noting that lines 235–378 are in the form of reported direct speech, as she gleefully recounts the way that she addressed her first husbands. This is the Wife at her most lively and playful, mocking her husbands and twisting their arguments in her favour. She never loses sight of her overall purpose, however. Near the end of this section she says that 'oon of us two moste bowen, douteless' (line 440). It is the final message of both her prologue and her tale that, in this battle for mastery, the man should always submit to the woman's will: '**And eek I praye Jhesu shorte hir lives / That wol nat be governed by hir wives**' (lines 1261–62).

Lines 452–502: Her fourth husband

In this section she describes her fourth husband, the first of her two 'badde' husbands.

Commentary: The fourth husband is given the epithet 'badde' because he is not under her control, and indeed he 'hadde a paramour' (line 454). She requites him for this by making him jealous – not through adultery ('nat of my body', line 485) but by flirting with other men. Note how careful she is here and elsewhere to avoid the condemnation that she is adulterous or in the wrong. She justifies her treatment of her fourth husband by saying that he was a 'revelour' (line 453) and that she has no sorrow at his death: 'It nis but wast to burye him preciously' (line 500). This is comically callous, but you may like to consider how far it reflects the fact that most marriages in this era were formed for economic rather than romantic reasons. This husband forms a thematic bridge between her first three husbands, who were easily dominated, and her fifth, who seeks to dominate her. The theme of 'maistrie' is thus gradually developed.

Lines 503–626: Her courtship with Jankin

Her fifth husband is Jankin, who has already been mentioned in line 303. He was an Oxford student (line 527), although at this point he has left university and is lodging with one of the Wife's friends, her 'gossib' (line 529). The three of them 'into the feeldes wente' (line 549), and she and Jankin had 'swich daliance' (line 565) that she arranges with him that 'if I were widwe, [he] sholde wedde me' (line 568). He is young, unlike her first three husbands, being just 'twenty winter oold' (line 600), and she is 'fourty, if I shal seye sooth' (line 601). She is captivated by his youth and physical charms.

Commentary: The difference between Jankin and her previous husbands is that he is young, and she marries him 'for love, and no richesse' (line 526). She flirts with him, and agrees to marry him even while her fourth husband is still alive. Once more she avoids a direct charge of adultery but, although she claims that she is just securing her future ('I was never withouten purveiance / Of mariage', lines 570–71), she is clearly smitten with him. There is an immensely comic moment when she describes how she stares at his legs even during her fourth husband's funeral:

> As help me God! Whan that I saugh him go
> After the beere, me thoughte he hadde a paire
> Of legges and of feet so clene and faire
> That al myn herte I yaf unto his hold.

(lines 596–99)

This passage suggests a softer and more sentimental side to the Wife of Bath, and builds thematic tension as the audience waits to hear what transpires between her and Jankin when they are married. You will notice that the disparity in ages has been reversed; he is the young man, marrying the 'old' and rich woman.

Lines 627–828: Jankin, her fifth husband

The final quarter of the Wife's prologue is taken up with her description of the relationship between her and Jankin. Much of this section (lines 641–787) consists of anti-feminist material that Jankin cites against her. She describes how she loses her temper, rips three leaves from the book and hits him. He hits her back, but regrets it immediately and asks for forgiveness. She grants it once he gives her total control, and they are happy afterwards.

Commentary: This is the heart of the Wife of Bath's prologue, and the centre of her crucial theme, 'maistrie' – that is, which partner shall have dominance within a marriage. This topic is dealt with in the 'Themes' section, on page 25

> **Build critical skills**
>
> To what extent do you agree that Chaucer presents Jankin as having similar motives for marrying the (no longer young) Wife as she had for marrying her old husbands?

Why does Chaucer insert this brief moment of marital subservience by the Wife (lines 630–31), given the discord that follows?

Taking it further ▶

By the time of the pilgrimage the Wife is once more a widow. Consider what might have happened to Jankin.

▲ An image of the Friar from a fourteenth-century manuscript

of this guide. She loves Jankin, which immediately gives him an advantage that her previous husbands have not had, and she cedes control totally to him:

> And to him yaf I al the lond and fee
> That evere was me yeven therbifoore.

(lines 630–31)

He, however, turns out to be more anti-feminist than any of the others, and as a scholar is able to read from his book numerous examples of women's failings (lines 669–787). This continues until she is pushed beyond endurance, and suddenly 'three leves have I plight / Out of his book' (lines 790–91). This symbolic defiance of male authority (and a powerful act of vandalism at a time when manuscripts were enormously rare and expensive) is the turning point in the prologue. She adds to it by punching him, and he retaliates by hitting her. This mistake shifts the balance of power in her favour, and his instant mortification gives her the advantage she needs. He grants her the 'maistrie' and 'soveraineetee' (line 818) in their marriage, and she 'made him brenne his book anon right tho' (line 816), thus symbolically destroying his male authority completely. Having achieved dominance, she says that they lived happily and she was 'kinde' (line 823) and 'also trewe' (line 825) to him. The Wife's whole prologue has led up to this thematic assertion that it is better for women to be in control.

Lines 829–56: The Friar and the Summoner

In an echo of the Pardoner's earlier interruption in lines 163–93, the Friar is so amazed by the Wife's garrulity that he laughs at her assertion that she is only now just about to begin: 'Now wol I seye my tale, if ye wol heere' (line 828). An argument develops between him and the Summoner, until the Host puts an end to it and asks the Wife to tell her tale.

Commentary: As with the Pardoner's interruption earlier, Chaucer introduces a dramatic interlude to mark the transition from the Wife's prologue to her tale. In giving the transition the form of an argument between the Friar and the Summoner, two pilgrims who cannot stand each other, Chaucer neatly exploits this conflict and lays the groundwork for further tales in the collection (lines 845–48). At long last (after 850 lines of prologue, as long as many of the stories in *The Canterbury Tales*) the Wife is ready to begin her tale, for which the pilgrims and Chaucer's audience have doubtless been impatiently waiting. The joke that 'this is a long preamble of a tale!' (line 831) is meant to make us think about what we have just experienced. The tale will only be half as long as its prologue; Chaucer clearly intends us to view the prologue as a major (or the major) component of his portrayal of the Wife and her views.

The Wife of Bath's Tale

By comparison with her prologue, the Wife of Bath's tale is short and more straightforward.

Lines 857–81: The introduction

The tale is set in the legendary time of King Arthur, 'manie hundred yeres ago' (line 863), when the country was 'fulfild of faierie' (line 859). The Wife contrasts this with her own modern time, when friars and other holy men have driven all the fairies away.

Commentary: The Wife begins her tale in the formal, once-upon-a-time style that we now associate with children's fairy stories, and indeed this appears to be a fairy story at the beginning. Early on, however (line 864), the Wife changes the tone and mood of the tale by introducing 'modern' friars, whose Christianity she says has driven the fairies out. The mood is further soured at the end of this section, when the Wife snidely accuses the friars of being incubi ('Ther is noon other incubus but he', line 880); incubi were malignant spirits that were supposed to have sexual intercourse with women while they were asleep and were (conveniently) often blamed for unwanted pregnancies. The Wife says that the friars seduce and dishonour women. Friars must have had a bad reputation in Chaucer's day, because he uses the same accusation in lines 208–14 of *The General Prologue*. The Wife's purpose is obviously to discredit men in general at the beginning of her tale, so that the crime that follows seems a common aspect of their behaviour.

▲ An image of the Summoner from a fourteenth-century manuscript

---

Context

The Wife sets her tale 'manie hundred yeres ago' in King Arthur's court. This was a common technique with medieval writers because King Arthur was such a popular legendary figure.

Lines 882–88: The knight rapes a young woman

In stark terms, the Wife describes the way that one of King Arthur's knights rapes a young maiden.

Commentary: This is the central event of the tale and provides the basis for all that follows. The Wife of Bath describes the rape in blunt terms:

> He saugh a maide walkinge him biforn,
> Of which maide anon, maugree hir heed,
> By verray force, he rafte hire maidenhed

(lines 886–88)

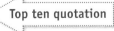

Top ten quotation

Context

The tale is a knightly romance, like the stories about King Arthur. It subverts the conventions of the genre, because instead of an honourable knight rescuing a damsel in distress, a dishonourable knight is 'rescued' by a foul hag. The basic story was already popular when Chaucer used it.

What makes the crime more awful is that it is committed by one of King Arthur's knights, against a young maiden he encounters as he travels. Everybody, in both medieval and modern audiences, would know that knights, and especially King Arthur's, were sworn to protect the innocent. Thus the Wife deliberately makes the knight's crime against the woman as bad as it can be, in order to place him in the worst possible moral position and to reinforce the impression she gives of what can be expected from male behaviour. Note that the knight is never named in the tale, as if to imply that he represents all men.

Taking it further ▶

Examine other examples of such challenges in literature and fairy tales. What is the main narrative purpose of such challenges? It would, in particular, be worth exploring *Sir Gawain and the Green Knight*, written by a contemporary of Chaucer's, which features a similar part-serious, part-comic task.

Lines 889–918: The knight's challenge

The knight is condemned to death, but is redeemed by 'the queene and othere ladies mo' (line 894). The queen then issues the challenge that he should discover 'what thing is it that wommen moost desiren' (line 905), and she grants him the traditional fairy-tale term of a year and a day to find the answer.

Commentary: The Wife immediately makes the man subject to the will of women, in keeping with her continuing theme. Normally it would be the king who would pass judgement, but King Arthur submits to his wife's will 'and yaf him to the queene' (line 897), to be 'al at her wille' (line 897). This latter phrase is important: once the knight has committed the crime of rape, he is permanently subject to the will of women, first the queen and her ladies, and later the old hag. It is not until he submits absolutely to be ruled by a woman, as Jankin does at the end of the prologue, that he can be redeemed and lead a happy life.

Lines 919–88: His search for an answer

The knight travels through the land on his quest, but cannot find two people who can agree on the answer (lines 922–23). He is offered numerous suggestions, and the Wife herself comments on some of these. But he cannot discern a single correct answer, and turns sorrowfully towards home at the end of his year away.

Commentary: The search for the answer to a challenge is a traditional medieval and fairy-tale quest theme, and as usual the knight does not come by the answer easily. In keeping with so much of the tale, however, Chaucer mixes the apparently conventional material with the personal approach of the Wife of

Bath. Instead of just listing the possible answers to the question in lines 925–28, the Wife contributes her own opinion in lines 929–31:

> Somme seyde that oure hertes been most esed
> Whan that we been yflatered and yplesed.
> He gooth ful ny the sothe, I wol nat lie.

Lines 989–1013: He meets the old hag

The knight encounters a group of 24 dancing ladies, who then mysteriously disappear (lines 989–96). They are replaced by a foul-looking old lady, the supernatural 'loathly lady' of this and many other medieval stories. He speaks to her politely (lines 1005–08) – a significant contrast to his treatment of the maiden he met earlier. She says she will tell him the answer, but in return makes him promise to do the next thing that she asks; the knight agrees.

Commentary: The fairy-tale nature of the narrative is resumed as the knight encounters a supernatural group of ladies – presumably fairies – dancing 'under a forest side' (line 990), a traditional setting for mysterious and magical encounters. This is important because the tale now takes on a supernatural aspect with the introduction of the enchanted hag, whose enchantment cannot be broken until the knight has submitted to her will. The Wife is careful here to put the woman in complete command of the knight's fate, and to make him meekly accept it. He has to promise to carry out the next thing she asks of him, without knowing what that is. It is worthwhile to compare the tale here to the other known medieval versions of the story. The changes that Chaucer makes are summarised at the end of this section (on p.19), and are most instructive. The significant feature at this point is that the knight's options are taken away from him. To promise obedience without knowing what is being promised is always dangerous, but the knight has no choice. If he fails to answer the queen's question satisfactorily, he will die. Note that he makes the promise to the hag without even querying how she can know the correct answer. This is not realistic, but the Wife makes it this way to emphasise his submission.

Lines 1014–45: The knight's answer

Having gained his promise of obedience the hag whispers to the knight the answer to the question and they set off back to Arthur's court. The knight reveals the answer to be that women desire 'sovereinetee' (line 1038) and 'maistrie' over men. Not a single woman in the court disagrees with this, and the knight is granted his life.

Commentary: The knight is thus enabled to answer the queen's question when he returns to the court, and in traditional fairy-tale manner is saved from certain death at the last minute. The fairy-tale style of the story meshes with the evidence from experience that the Wife has given in her prologue. His answer

TASK

Consider carefully what Chaucer achieves by allowing the Wife's personal voice to break through into this kind of conventional narrative. To what extent does it lessen the impact of the story, or contribute further to our understanding of the Wife and her attitudes?

Build critical skills

To what extent does Chaucer encourage his audience to sympathise with the knight here? In your response, consider how Chaucer's techniques throughout the tale have reduced the knight to a level of extreme submissiveness.

is seen to be thematically inevitable in the context of the whole of *The Wife of Bath's Prologue* and *Tale*:

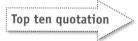
Top ten quotation

> Wommen desiren to have sovereinetee
> As wel over hir housbond as hir love,
> And for to been in maistrie him above.

(lines 1038–40)

Note the presence of the key word 'maistrie', which the Wife used at the end of her prologue (line 818) and which will recur at the end of the tale (line 1236) (see 'Themes', p.25 of this guide). Note also that the hag's answer states that women desire dominance over both their husbands and their lovers; as so often, the hag here seems to be a mouthpiece for the views of the Wife herself. It is for you to judge how far this is true, and how far the hag has other aspects that take her beyond this simple identification. You will want to look particularly at the passage below on 'gentillesse' in lines 1104–218.

Lines 1046–103: The marriage

The hag immediately demands that the knight keeps his promise and fulfils her next request. To his dismay, she insists that they get married. The knight is horrified and begs her to choose something else, but she is adamant. They get married, but on their wedding night he is in torment, while she lies there 'smiling everemo' (line 1086). She queries his lack of passion, and he condemns her for being loathsome, old and of low birth (not a noblewoman).

Commentary: This passage is richly comic. The humour ranges from the predicament the knight finds himself in, to the thematic conflict between the man's and the woman's will. In this section the more formal story-telling mode is replaced by the kind of realistic comic dialogue that features so strongly in the Wife's prologue. In contrast to the knight's earlier courteous speech to the lady (lines 1005–08), the Wife of Bath here permits him to protest about his situation:

> Thou art so loothly, and so oold also,
> And therto comen of so lough a kinde.

(lines 1100–01)

This merely places him at a further moral disadvantage. The Wife adds to the comedy by emphasising the joylessness of the marriage ceremony (lines 1073–82), and his wife's sarcastic surprise at his behaviour when they go to bed (lines 1087–90). The point is sharpened with her reference to 'the lawe of King Arthures hous' (line 1089). The obvious irony is that he raped a young woman without a thought, but is now unwilling to have sexual intercourse with his legitimate wife. The section ends with her tantalising offer to 'amende al this' (line 1106) – an offer the knight cannot understand because he is unaware that she is supernatural. He is trapped in a 'realistic' situation; the audience can enjoy his suffering because they are aware of the fairy-tale dimension to the story.

Lines 1104–218: 'Gentillesse'

With another change of tone, the Wife delays the denouement of the tale by introducing a formal digression on the nature of 'gentillesse'. The lady chastises the knight for his discourteous manners, and states that truly noble behaviour is a gift from God, not an accident of birth.

Commentary: The term 'gentillesse' most naturally translates as 'gentility' – the courteousness and polite manners expected of a person of noble or 'gentle' birth.

The digression occurs at a dramatic point in the tale. The knight has just asserted in forceful terms that 'it wol nat been amended nevere mo' (line 1099) – note the intensifying double negative. His wife immediately replies that 'I koude amende al this, / if that me liste' (lines 1106–07), an intriguing claim given the knight's despair. Chaucer (or the Wife of Bath) now delays the resolution of the situation for well over a hundred lines – a quarter of the tale – thus keeping the audience (and the knight) in suspense. In this way the lady asserts further her power over the knight because she withholds her decision to relieve his anguish until she has delivered her discourse. The knight has no option but to listen meekly.

In this passage the lady picks up the knight's reference to her supposedly low-born status ('so lough a kinde', line 1101) and assumes he means to contrast it with his own nobility. She proceeds to deny the connection between birth and behaviour and claims that 'gentillesse' comes directly from God: 'Crist wole we claime of him oure gentillesse' (line 1117). She repeats this point several times, for example, **For gentillesse cometh fro God allone** (line 1162) and concludes 'That he is gentil that dooth gentil dedis' (line 1170).

In lamenting his own lot, the knight has been deeply offensive to his wife:

> Thou art so loothly, and so oold also,
> And therto comen of so lough a kinde.
>
> (lines 1100–01)

No woman likes being called ugly or old, or low-born – and this is the woman he has just married, however reluctantly. The situation is comic, but the Wife of Bath has made the knight outspoken in order to put him yet further in the wrong. To all his previous crimes is added that of discourtesy, which for a nobleman would be a grievous failing. The Wife allows the lady to take full advantage of this with her lecture, and gives her the moral high ground. She has behaved well to him and has saved his life; he has treated her poorly in return, and disgraced his knightly name.

As far as the Wife of Bath is concerned the lecture on 'gentillesse' adds a final dimension to her complex condemnation of male behaviour. By outlining what

---

TASK

Examine the knight's state of mind as he 'walweth and he turneth' in mental agony and consider how far we sympathise with him at this point. Is this a naturalistic moment, or done for comic effect?

Top ten quotation

genteel behaviour should be, she emphasises the way in which men fall short of such ideals.

Chaucer's purpose may be rather different. The loathly lady's discourse on virtue can be seen as reflecting on the Wife herself, as well as on her ostensible targets. If 'gentillesse' is a virtue, and is not linked to birth, then the Wife of Bath should be able to behave according to its principles as well as anyone. That she does not can be seen as a condemnation of her, which is placed by Chaucer as the final feature in the overall sweep of her prologue and tale.

It is often tempting to see the loathly lady as a kind of further persona of the Wife of Bath, a projection of her character that enables her to get the better of yet another man – and in this case, one of King Arthur's knights. The speech on gentillesse suggests the limits of this view. The tenor and sentiments of the speech are not the Wife's – it preaches the qualities of humility and virtuous living. Its conclusion is at odds with all that the Wife has said in her prologue:

> Yet may the hye God, and so hope I,
> Grante me grace to liven vertuously.

(lines 1173–74)

As elsewhere, the erudition displayed in the speech is Chaucer's rather than the Wife's. The references to Dante, Boethius, Seneca and Walter Map show his learning rather than hers, and the lecture and moral are ultimately his. It is important always to remember this distinction between narrator and author.

The distinction is made greater when the wider context of *The Canterbury Tales* is considered. In particular, *The Franklin's Tale* – the last of the so-called marriage group – centres on the concept of 'gentillesse' and what constitutes right behaviour within marriage. It is evident that Chaucer's preoccupation with the issue extends beyond the immediate context of *The Wife of Bath's Tale*, and so the character of the Wife of Bath is subservient to the wider needs of the author.

Lines 1219–64: The resolution

The final section closes both the tale and *The Wife of Bath's Prologue* and *Tale* as a whole. The lady gives the knight a cruel choice between having her ugly and faithful, or beautiful and potentially faithless. In the analogues (see p.35 of this guide) the hag turns into a beautiful woman before the knight has to make his choice, and usually she reveals that she is under an enchantment. In Chaucer's version the hag keeps absolute power to herself by failing to allow the knight to have any of this information, and he remains in torment. The knight inevitably grants her the 'maistrie' (line 1236), and only then is rewarded by her transformation into a beautiful and loyal wife. The Wife of Bath ends with a final personal and characteristic jibe against husbands who will not be subservient to their wives.

Commentary: The Wife of Bath's prologue and her tale are a unified construction, like a piece of music with a single theme that is explored through a series of variations. As in music, particular phrases are repeated in order to give structure and coherence to the whole work, and to emphasise particular ideas. A comparison of the ending of the Wife's prologue with the ending of her tale is instructive about Chaucer's craft and purpose. This can be seen by pairing quotations, as follows:

> He yaf me al the bridel in myn hond,
> To han the governance of hous and lond
>
> (lines 813–14)

> I put me in youre wise governance
>
> (line 1231)

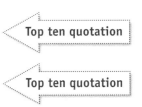

> And whan that I hadde geten unto me,
> By maistrie, al the soverainetee
>
> (lines 817–18)

> Thanne have I gete of yow maistrie
>
> (line 1236)

> Do as thee lust the terme of al thy lyf;
> Keep thyn honour, and keep eek myn estaat
>
> (lines 820–21)

> Cheseth youreself which may be moost plesance,
> And moost honour to yow and me also.
>
> (lines 1232–33)

> God helpe me so, I was to him as kinde
> As any wyf from Denmark unto Inde,
> And also trewe, and so was he to me.
>
> (lines 823–25)

> I prey to God that I moote sterven wood,
> But I to yow be also good and trewe
> As evere was wyf, sin that the world was newe.
> And but I be to-morn as fair to seene
> As any lady, emperice, or queene,
> That is bitwixe the est and eke the west
>
> (lines 1242–47)

Structurally, the close parallels between the endings of the prologue and the tale act to signify the unity of the work; the audience is intended to consider the two elements as a single continuous piece. The parallelism also shows that the apparently rambling nature of the Wife's prologue is an artifice. Every step in it is calculated to lead up to the points made at the end, in the way that a symphonic movement builds to a grand conclusion. The tale acts as the development of the theme in another key, but returns to the dominant mode at the end to round off the entire work and provide a satisfying sense of completeness.

Thematically, the ending of the tale serves to reinforce the Wife's arguments from the prologue. The relation of her own experiences leads to the inexorable conclusion that women should have 'maistrie'. The tale works in a literary story-telling mode, but comes to precisely the same conclusion. The Wife's intention is clear: whatever the circumstances, she says, it is better for women to have control.

It is clear that she means her audience to understand that the loathly lady of the tale and the Wife of the prologue are one voice in two different guises. The paralleling of phraseology, with colloquial terms as close as 'God helpe me so' (line 823) and 'I prey to God' (line 1242), is deliberate and forceful.

The Wife of Bath's Tale and its analogues

An analogue is a version of a story or text that is similar (analogous) to another one. Folk tales and songs, for example, frequently occur in different forms with major or minor variations. The tale that the Wife tells is well known and exists in various forms. There are summaries of the three main analogues on page 35 of this guide. Chaucer deliberately changes crucial aspects of the tale to suit the Wife's character and beliefs. The most significant alterations are listed together below, so that you can see the overall effect of the changes. Every one of the alterations puts the man in a worse light and puts the women in greater control. Chaucer subtly modifies the circumstances so that the knight, guilty of rape at the start, is forced to submit to women's control at every stage of the tale.

1 **The knight is a member of King Arthur's court, and is never named.** As one of Arthur's knights, the man should be chivalrous. Leaving him anonymous diminishes him and makes him a representative male.

2 **The knight rapes a young maiden at the beginning of the tale.** This is the most explicit indicator of male dominance. The fact that it is committed by one of Arthur's knights makes the crime more heinous; they were famed for protecting 'damsels in distress', not for assaulting them.

3 **The queen intervenes to save the knight's life.** Power over the fate of the man is immediately placed in female hands.

> **TASK**
>
> Chaucer's tale, which seems so original to us, would have been familiar to many in his audience. How much difference does that make? How did your own reaction to the tale change between your first reading of it and subsequent re-readings?

4   **Before he meets the ugly old woman, the knight first encounters 24 beautiful ladies dancing.** This adds to the fairy-tale quality of the narrative. It strengthens the suggestion that women have the power – and 24 is a magical number.

5   **The knight is not permitted to try other answers, only the hag's.** Chaucer continuously removes choice from the knight. In the analogues, quite comically, whole books of answers are drawn up and tried before the knight reluctantly resorts to the hag's answer. Here, the knight is not given the option of trying alternatives.

6   **The hag accompanies him back to Arthur's court.** The woman exerts further control by staying with the knight throughout.

7   **On their wedding night, his wife makes a long speech about 'gentillesse'.** The woman is seen to be reasonable and honourable, in direct contrast to the knight. She preaches a meek and courteous mode of behaviour, which the knight has conspicuously failed to show.

8   **The knight has to make his choice on their wedding night, before he sees his wife in her beautiful form.** The knight's 'reward' is delayed, and the woman does not cede her position by allowing him to see that she can be beautiful.

9   **Chaucer alters the choice the knight has to make.** In the analogues, the husband chooses whether to have his wife beautiful during the day or during the night – a tricky decision. In Chaucer's version, the knight is offered the choice of an ugly but faithful wife, or a beautiful one who may not be faithful to him. This is the crucial change. It introduces a moral element into the tale by making the knight choose between virtue and pleasure; it is a much sharper question than in the analogues.

10 **There is no suggestion that the woman has been enchanted by a wicked stepmother.** The hag is in command of her own destiny. The assumption is that she has transformed herself in order to test and gain power over the man.

TASK

Examine the sections of the text identified in this list. In each case, exactly what has Chaucer gained by making the changes?

Themes

Target your thinking

- What do you regard as the key theme in *The Wife of Bath's Prologue* and *Tale*? (**AO1**)
- How important is it that *The Wife of Bath's Prologue* and *Tale* is just one of *The Canterbury Tales*? (**AO3**, **AO4**)
- In your view, does Chaucer suggest that 'experience' or 'auctoritee' is more important? (**AO5**)

Experience and 'auctoritee'

Top ten quotation

Build critical skills

How do you think a medieval audience might have reacted to the use of the word 'Experience' as the opening word of the text?

'**Auctoritee**' (line 1) – or authority – is a key word for the understanding of medieval texts. Medieval people had the utmost respect for authorities, and especially the absolute authority of the Bible and other scriptures. In her prologue, the Wife of Bath sets out to discuss the institution of marriage (for her, the 'wo that is in mariage'), and this is in itself unusual because Chaucer places the analysis in the mouth of a woman. Usually, the viewpoint would be that of a man, and the argument would proceed almost entirely by quoting (invariably male) written authorities and sources. Instead, the Wife of Bath opens her prologue with the word 'Experience'. The importance of her doing this, and the challenge it represents to traditional 'auctoritee', cannot be overemphasised. She claims that she does not need to rely on 'auctoritee' or even to accept that her life should be regulated by traditional doctrines.

Ironically, despite this opening claim, the Wife immediately starts to cite 'auctoritees', beginning with Christ's attendance at a marriage in Cana, and continues to cite a huge array of examples and authorities throughout her prologue. The whole of *The Wife of Bath's Prologue* and *Tale* thus becomes a conflict between the traditional claims of authority and the practical claims of experience. It is the student's task to decide where the balance lies when the Wife has finished.

CRITICAL VIEW

James Winny, in his original 1965 Cambridge University Press edition of the text, claims that 'she has overthrown the prohibitive morality of the medieval Church and planted her own pragmatic doctrine on the ruins' (p.15). This is quite a claim and one that Winny toned down slightly for his revised 1994 edition, replacing the word 'overthrown' with 'contested' but retaining the gist of the argument. For Winny, her statement that she has had five 'housbondes at chirche dore' gives her practical authority – experience – to set against the theoretical writings of ecclesiastical scholars, who would have been celibate. When she says 'this gentil text kan I wel understonde', it is her practical experiences as a married woman that, for Winny, make her viewpoint persuasive.

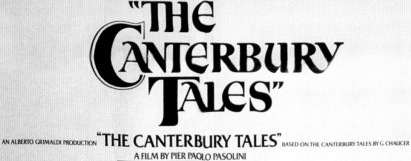

▲ Still from the 1972 flim *I Racconti di Canterbury*, starring Laura Betti as the Wife

The words of the text, of course, are not the Wife's but Chaucer's. It is his erudition on display, and his choice of how the Wife is presented to his audience. The same line that James Winny (see 'Critical view' box on page 20) believes shows the superiority of her practical experience ('this gentil text kan I wel understonde') is taken by D.W. Robertson (see 'Critical view' box on page 21) precisely to show her *lack* of understanding. The 'gentil text' she is referring to is God's injunction in Genesis to 'wexe and multiplie', and this is the Church's traditional view of the purpose of marriage. Yet the Wife of Bath has no interest in this aspect; she never refers to having children, and is solely interested in the sexual act itself, not in its outcomes. In this sense, she is an embodiment of the sin of Lust. Robertson claims that Chaucer offers a 'scathing denunciation of such understanding'.

The contrast between Winny's views and Robertson's is illuminating and instructive. Winny's approach is based on his view of the Wife as a fully realised human individual – 'her indiscretions and shortcomings do not stand as types of moral weakness, but as details of a complicated personality' (p.5). This is a modern reading, and credits Chaucer with creating a modern kind of psychological portrait. As a result, Winny claims, she presents 'a case for the kind of sexual freedom which she has chosen instinctively throughout her life' (pp.14–15). The choice of the word 'instinctively' is telling; Winny treats her as if she were a real human being offering us her life story.

Robertson, by contrast, takes a completely medieval view of Chaucer's craft and purpose. He concludes his discussion: 'Alisoun of Bath is not a "character" in the modern sense at all, but an elaborate iconographic figure designed to show the manifold implications of an attitude' (p.330). That is to say, she is a literary construct, a device created by Chaucer for the purpose of outlining – and ultimately rejecting – a point of view.

The contrast between the two critics is stark, and each reader must decide which has greater validity. Despite the opposed positions, it is possible to assert that both are right. Robertson presents the medieval context, an interpretation based on the way that art and literature operated in the fourteenth century. Winny presents a twentieth-century response, which is valid if *The Canterbury Tales* is taken as a living work of art, independent of its historical origins.

This leads on to questions about how far any work of art needs to be understood in terms of its original contexts, and how far each generation interprets art according to its own standards and concerns.

Winny's assertion that the Wife 'has overthrown the prohibitive morality of the medieval Church' seems extreme, an argument built with hindsight and a Romantic, perhaps even a 1960s', perspective of admiration for rebel figures. Chaucer's audience could enjoy listening to her arguments and attitudes, and even agree with much of what she says about the tribulations of married life, without losing their own respect for 'auctoritee' or traditional teachings. Rather, the Wife emerges as somebody who demonstrates exactly the vices of an unruly wife that the Church condemned. She might be fun to listen to, but that does not mean you have to agree with what she has to say. Winny actually admits this: 'she is herself a conspicuous example of all the wifely vices imputed to her sex' (p.20). When her arguments are examined minutely, many seem simply erroneous.

Context

The medieval tendency to respect authority contrasts with the tendency of the modern mind to challenge authority. In part this is a difference between a religious age where divine revelation was all-important, and a scientific age where everything is subject to enquiry and scrutiny.

Robertson's argument is more measured and conducted at length through numerous examples. It has clear validity in a medieval context. The issue is how far Chaucer can be said, even unconsciously, to be moving beyond the entirely traditional medieval literary mode of art as instructional, and presaging the more humanistic and naturalistic approach of the Renaissance. This is an issue that cannot be easily resolved, and remains a matter of judgement.

TASK

Do you regard Winny's view of the Wife as more convincing than Robertson's, or less so?

Anti-feminism

Much of the material in *The Wife of Bath's Prologue* derives from anti-feminist writing. The condemnation of women is a regrettably strong feature of Catholic writing in the Middle Ages, inspired by the belief that the Fall of Man in Genesis was caused by Eve, and confirmed by the misogynistic attitude of St Paul in the New Testament, who argued specifically that people should not marry. Given this biblical anti-feminist basis, it is no surprise that later writers emphasised the weakness and fickleness of women. Chaucer invented the character of the Wife of Bath in order to explore some of the issues surrounding this anti-feminist bias in the fourteenth century. It is of course ironic that the Wife should quote so many sources of this kind when she is trying to advocate the supremacy of women, but that is part of Chaucer's technique. One of the key sources is Theophrastus' *Liber aureolus de nuptiis* (*Golden Book of Marriage*). Compare this extract from Theophrastus with lines 235–315 of *The Wife of Bath's Prologue*:

A wise man, therefore, must not take a wife. For in the first place his study of philosophy will be hindered, and it is impossible for anyone to attend to his books and his wife. Wives want many things – costly dresses, gold, jewels, great outlay, maid-servants, all kinds of furniture, litters and gilded coaches. Then come curtain-lectures the livelong night: she complains that one lady goes out better-dressed than she; that another is looked up to by all. 'I am a poor despised nobody at the ladies' assemblies.' 'Why did you ogle that creature next door?' 'Why were you talking to the maid?' 'What did you bring from the market?' 'I am not allowed to have a single friend or companion.' There may be in some neighbouring city the wisest of teachers; but if we have a wife we can neither leave her behind nor take the burden with us. To support a poor wife is hard; to put up with a rich one is torture. Notice, too, that in the case of a wife you cannot pick or choose; you must take her as you find her. If she has a bad temper, or is a fool, if she has a blemish, or is proud, or has bad breath, whatever her fault may be – all this we learn after marriage. Horses, asses, cattle, even slaves of the smallest worth, clothes, kettles, wooden seats, cups and earthenware pitchers, are first tried and then bought: a wife is the only thing that is not shown before she is married, for fear she may not give satisfaction.

Our gaze must always be directed to her face, and we must always praise her beauty: if you look at another woman, she thinks that she is

Build critical skills

How far do you think a medieval audience would have recognised the portrayal of relationships that Theophrastus offers?

out of favour. She must be called 'my lady', her birthday must be kept, we must swear by her health and wish that she may survive us. Respect must be paid to the nurse, to the nursemaid, to the father's slave; to the foster-child, to the handsome hanger-on, to the curled darling who manages her affairs, and to the eunuch who ministers to the safe indulgence of her lust; names which are only a cloak for adultery. Upon whomsoever she sets her heart, they must have her love, though they want her not. If you give her the management of the whole house, you must yourself be her slave. If you reserve something for yourself, she will think you are not loyal to her; but she will turn to strife and hatred, and unless you quickly take care, she will have the poison ready…

(Translated from the Latin by W.H. Fremantle, *The Principal Works of St Jerome* (1893))

The Wife borrows the views of Theophrastus in order to make fun of them. He attacks women; she takes his words and uses them for her own attack on anti-feminist attitudes and her luckless early husbands, who appear to have been unable to withstand the barrage. She accuses her early husbands of accusing her unfairly, and makes out that they are being absurd:

> And if that she be fair, thou verray knave,
> Thou seist that every holour wol hir have.

(lines 253–54)

By making their claims appear unjustified, she is finally able to accuse them of harbouring false suspicions about her relationship with Jankin:

> Yet hastow caught a fals suspecioun.
> I wol him noght, thogh thou were deed tomorwe!

(lines 306–07)

She is clearly using attack as a form of defence, for Jankin will become her fifth husband.

Chaucer's purpose here is more debatable. The passage is highly comic, and the Wife's ranting is powerful and eloquent. The audience may enjoy the way she takes the fight to the 'enemy', her husbands, and they may share her view that misogynistic attitudes are appalling. Alternatively, they may laugh at her overwhelming personality and be glad, like the Pardoner in lines 166–68, that they have escaped her clutches. The more nervous of the pilgrims may remember her boast that she is even now looking for a sixth husband (line 45). The more austere and hostile listeners, whether on the pilgrimage or in Chaucer's audience, might feel that she exemplifies exactly the truth that Theophrastus sought to reveal, and that women are indeed to be avoided at all costs. Students must make up their own minds about how they wish to respond.

Another key area of *The Wife of Bath's Prologue* that should be examined is the list of specific anti-feminist examples quoted by Jankin in lines 713–64. At this point, technically, Chaucer the pilgrim is repeating the Wife of Bath's words, and she is referring to what her husband Jankin read out to her. In reality, the whole thing is written by Chaucer the author. The reader should expect complexity of effect and response here.

Lists of examples, or *exempla* in Latin, were extremely popular in medieval literature, and formed one of the mainstays of all writers and preachers. It is no surprise to see Chaucer, the Wife or Jankin using them.

Jankin's purpose is evident. He referred to numerous examples of 'wikked wives' (line 685) to prove beyond doubt that women are untrustworthy and inclined to evil deeds. He sought to annoy and overwhelm his wife through sheer weight of evidence. There are ten specific examples cited in lines 713–64, and these are followed by more general references in lines 765–87.

The Wife's purpose is equally clear. She is trying to demonstrate that Jankin was grossly unreasonable and vindictive, and she therefore justifies her response of ripping the leaves out of the book as being because she had been provoked beyond endurance.

Chaucer the pilgrim, of course, is merely repeating the Wife's words, and we are given no impression of what he thinks about her. He is invisible in this part of *The Canterbury Tales*.

It is Chaucer the author whose intentions need close consideration. He can be seen as endorsing the Wife's anger at the prolonged bullying of her by her husband; or he may be seen as embodying in the Wife exactly the kind of vices that Jankin complained about, therefore justifying the misogynistic stance that he took. Both responses to the text can be defended, and your choice will depend on your overall reading of *The Wife of Bath's Prologue* and *Tale*.

> **TASK**
> Consider the difference between Chaucer's age and our own in terms of attitudes towards and treatment of women. What specific changes can you identify?

'Maistrie'

'Maistrie' – mastery – is the key theme of *The Wife of Bath's Prologue* and *Tale*, and is the theme that binds the prologue and tale into a unified entity. Thematically it is a constant obsession for the Wife in her prologue, and is at the core of the tale that she offers as an *exemplum* of her beliefs.

The concept of 'maistrie' is used by the Wife specifically in terms of the relationships between men and women, especially within marriage. She believes that one of the partners must be dominant, and sets out to prove that this should be the woman.

The word 'maistrie' itself is used three times in *The Wife of Bath's Prologue* and *Tale*, in lines 818, 1040 and 1236. Significantly, the first of these usages is at the end of her prologue, and the other two at the end of her tale. These placements are significant because they act as conclusions to the Wife's argument in both *The Wife of Bath's Prologue* and her *Tale*.

Chaucer already signals the Wife's character in her portrait in *The General Prologue*, where he comments that she had 'on hir feet a paire of spores sharpe' (line 475). Throughout her prologue she metaphorically goads her husbands and shows them who is in control.

From an early stage she makes it perfectly clear that she seeks domination over her husbands, rather than equality:

Top ten quotation

> An housbonde I wol have, I wol nat lette,
> Which shal be bothe my dettour and my thral.
>
> (lines 154–55)

She revels in her sexual mastery over her first three husbands:

> I sette hem so a-werke, by my fey,
> That many a night they songen 'weilawey!'
>
> (lines 215–16)

Her long description of how she berated them (lines 235–378) culminates with her conclusion:

> Lordinges, right thus, as ye have understonde,
> Baar I stifly mine olde housbondes on honde.
>
> (lines 379–80)

She also dominated her fourth husband, despite his behaviour:

> There was no wight, save God and he, that wiste,
> In many wise, how soore I him twiste.
>
> (lines 493–94)

But all this is a mere prelude to the conflict between her and her fifth husband, Jankin. She sets him up as a worthy adversary, able to argue his own side and condemn her with all his anti-feminist sources. This is done so that his defeat, when it comes, is absolute and the Wife's triumph supreme:

> And that he seyde, 'Myn owene trewe wyf,
> Do as thee lust the terme of al thy lyf...'
>
> (lines 819–20)

This would be ample to demonstrate the single-minded intent of the Wife of Bath, but she then goes on to repeat the theme exactly in her tale. Again she sets up a strong adversary – an Arthurian knight who asserts his 'maistrie' by raping a young woman. The knight is progressively humbled throughout the tale, until he too submits:

Top ten quotation

> My lady and my love, and wyf so deere,
> I put me in youre wise governance …
>
> (lines 1230–31)

The fact that both men voluntarily submit emphasises that the women's 'maistrie' is total.

It is important to view the whole of the Wife's argument within the context of medieval views on marriage, but it is also necessary to consider its placement within Chaucer's treatment of marriage in several of *The Canterbury Tales* – the so-called marriage group. Medieval England was a Catholic Christian country, and marriage was one of the central Catholic sacraments. The most holy state was chastity – living without sexual relationships, like a monk or nun. The alternative was marriage – a single partnership between a man and a woman for their entire lifetime. Sex outside the marriage – adultery – or before marriage was a deadly sin and meant eternal damnation of the soul. Divorce was not permitted, although in exceptional circumstances marriages could be annulled. Within a marriage, the man was the master and the wife vowed obedience to him.

All this was in line with the patriarchal nature of religion and society. Almost all rulers were men. The vast majority of women had subservient positions and rarely had opportunity to express themselves or act independently (although, as ever, there were exceptions). Women could not be priests and were debarred from universities. Women were often despised as weak, an attitude deriving ultimately from the story of Adam and Eve in Genesis, where Eve succumbed to the Devil's temptation and then tempted Adam.

Chaucer's 'marriage group' of tales presents a variety of marriages and a number of attitudes towards marriage. He clearly intended his audience to debate what constituted a suitable relationship within marriage, and *The Wife of Bath's Prologue* and *Tale* offers one extreme of this continuum. The Wife's insistence on female dominance is at the opposite end to the behaviour of 'patient' Griselda in *The Clerk's Tale*, who undergoes fearful treatment at the hands of her husband and stands as the representative type of pure Christian and marital obedience.

TASK

Examine the 'Contexts' section on the 'marriage group' of tales, on page 65 of this guide. How does *The Wife of Bath's Prologue* and *Tale* fit into this discussion?

'Gentillesse'

The concepts indicated by the word 'gentillesse' preoccupied many medieval writers, and Chaucer particularly. In the common usage of the fourteenth century, the word primarily meant nobility of birth and/or inherited wealth (the two were usually connected). In this sense, 'gentillesse' equates to the later word gentility, which gave rise to the English word gentleman. Since wealth could easily be lost, however, and since everyone is ultimately descended from common parents (Adam and Eve), the term could have only a limited bearing. Philosophers (like Boethius in his *Consolation of Philosophy*) and other writers therefore tended to look beyond the superficial attributes of birth towards the essential characteristics of a person. 'Gentillesse' became associated with moral qualities, aspects of a person's virtue. It is in this sense that we find it in the works of writers like Chaucer and his friend John Gower. Most notably, it occurs in *The Parson's Tale*, which concludes *The Canterbury Tales* and is mainly a sermon about the seven deadly sins. The Parson, the most perfect of all the pilgrims, has this to say:

> Now been ther generale signes of gentillesse,
> As eschewynge of vice and ribaudye and servage
> Of synne, in word, in werk, and contenaunce;
> And usynge vertu, curteisye, and clennesse, and
> To be liberal, that is to seyn, large by mesure;
> For thilke that passeth mesure is folie and
> Synne.

'Vertu, curteisye, and clennesse' are the key concepts that underpin the word 'gentillesse' as it is used in *The Wife of Bath's Tale* (lines 1104–218). 'Vertu' means the pursuit of all the virtues, such as prudence, temperance, kindness and humility. These virtues were often seen as the opposites of the seven deadly sins. 'Curteisye' means courteous behaviour, that is the right treatment of others. 'Clennesse' means purity, both in conscience and in behaviour. Taken as a whole, the idea of 'gentillesse' can therefore be seen as the ideal not merely for a nobleman, but for any true Christian. The Wife of Bath uses the word in her tale as a means for the old hag to lecture and castigate the knight, who did, it should be remembered, rape a woman at the start of the tale and is now behaving discourteously to his new wife. The effect of the word's use in the tale is complex. The old hag's purpose is clear: she wants to show the knight how badly he is behaving. The Wife of Bath wishes this too, but she perhaps wants to indicate that all men are at fault because they do not live up to the ideals contained in the word 'gentillesse'. Chaucer's intentions, as so often, are more sophisticated. We understand the ideals that are being advocated, but we are conscious that they apply as much to women as to men. When applied to the Wife of Bath herself, it is evident that she is signally lacking in all the qualities signified by 'gentillesse'. She does not show 'vertu, curteisye, and clennesse', she 'passeth mesure', and can be judged against the standards that the Parson has set up as the ideal.

Characters

Target your thinking

- How far is your response to the Wife conditioned by your attitudes to feminism? (**AO1**)
- How far does the tale add to the understanding of the Wife that you gained from her prologue? (**AO2**)
- How far is the Wife of Bath more than a caricature? (**AO5**)

The Wife

The Wife in *The General Prologue*

Even if you are studying only *The Wife of Bath's Prologue* and *Tale* as a text, it is essential to examine the description of the Wife in *The General Prologue* as well. This is because the Wife is one of the most completely realised characters in *The Canterbury Tales*, and Chaucer moulds her prologue and tale carefully to suit the character he has set up in advance.

This is how the Wife of Bath is introduced in *The General Prologue* (lines 447–78). The modernised English version (on the right) is entirely literal, and is given to help clarify the meaning of the passage.

TASK

Why did Chaucer allow *The Wife of Bath's Prologue* and *Tale* to be so dominated by its narrator?

> **Context**
>
> In the Middle Ages, Bath was a centre for the wool industry and was famous for its tightly woven broadcloth. The Cotswold Hills were home to flocks of sheep, which provided the wool, and the nearby port of Bristol increased the opportunities for trade.

1 near	A good wif was ther of biside[1] Bathe	There was a goodwife (woman) from near Bath
2 somewhat	But she was somdel[2] deef, and that was scathe[3].	Who was somewhat deaf, which was a pity.
3 pity	Of clooth-makyng she hadde swich an haunt[4],	At cloth-making she had such a skill
4 skill	She passed hem of Ypres and of Gaunt.	That she surpassed those of Ypres and Ghent.
	In al the parisshe wif ne was ther noon	In all the parish there was no woman
	That to the offrynge bifore hire sholde goon;	Who should precede her in making the offering;

And if ther dide, certeyn so wrooth was she,

That she was out of alle charitee.

5 texture   Hir coverchiefs ful fyne weren of ground[5];

I dorste swere they weyeden ten pound

That on a Sonday weren upon hir heed.

Hir hosen weren of fyn scarlet reed,

Ful streite yteyd, and shoes ful moyste and newe.

Boold was hir face, and fair, and reed of hewe.

She was a worthy womman al hir lyve:

Housbondes at chirche dore she hadde fyve,

Withouten oother compaignye in youthe,—

But therof nedeth nat to speke as nowthe.

And thries hadde she been at Jerusalem;

6 foreign   She hadde passed many a straunge[6] strem;

At Rome she hadde been, and at Boloigne,

In Galice at Seint-Jame, and at Coloigne.

She koude muchel of wandrynge by the weye.

Gat-tothed was she, soothly for to seye.

Upon an amblere esily she sat,

Ywympled wel, and on hir heed an hat

7 types   As brood as is a bokeler[7] or a targe[7];
of shield

A foot-mantel aboute hir hipes large,

And on hir feet a paire of spores sharpe.

In felaweshipe wel koude she laughe and

8 chat   carpe[8].

Of remedies of love she knew per chaunce,

For she koude of that art the olde daunce.

And if anyone did, she was so angry,

That it put her out of all charity.

Her kerchiefs were of very fine texture;

I dare swear they weighed ten pounds

That she wore on her head on a Sunday.

Her hose were of fine scarlet red,

Tightly laced, and her shoes shiny and new.

Her face was bold, and fair, and red of hue.

She was a worthy woman all her life:

She had married five husbands at the church door,

Not counting other company in her youth—

But we don't need to speak of that now.

Three times had she been to Jerusalem;

She had crossed many foreign streams;

She had been to Rome, and Bologna (or Boulogne),

To Santiago in Spain, and to Cologne.

She knew a lot about wandering by the way.

She was gap-toothed, to tell the truth.

She sat easily on an ambler,

Well wimpled, and on her head a hat

As broad as a buckler or a target;

She had a foot-mantle about her large hips,

And on her feet a pair of sharp spurs.

In company she knew how to laugh and jest.

She knew about love remedies,

Because she knew all about that old game.

The Wife of Bath, then, is a large, flamboyant, gap-toothed woman with a bold, sanguine or ruddy complexion. She is rather deaf. She wears bright and prominent clothes – huge headgear, tightly laced red hosiery, shiny new shoes and sharp spurs. She has had a lot of experience of life for a medieval woman. She has had five husbands (and is currently a widow) besides 'other company in youth', and has travelled all round Europe on pilgrimages. She insists on social precedence in church, presumably as the highest-ranked woman in her parish. She is quick to anger, but also loves laughing and company. She knows all about love and love remedies. She is a skilled cloth maker.

The physical description immediately provokes responses about the character of the Wife. She is a brazen, pushy woman, with high self-regard and a fondness for the company of men. Attempting to translate some of the lines reveals ambiguities that are clearly deliberate – there is a gap between the literal and metaphorical readings. The most famous is the phrase 'wandringe by the weye'. Does this mean simply that she has travelled a lot, or is there an implication that she strays from the right path? Similarly, her knowledge of love remedies might simply indicate a bit of potion-making and being an agony aunt, but there could be a suggestion that she undertakes abortions. Her youthful behaviour could be harmless, or it might be sinful. In this context, her apparently pitiable (physical) deafness could suggest a parallel spiritual deafness, being unwilling or unable to heed proper Christian teaching. Even the gap between her teeth would have been seen in medieval times as a sign of lasciviousness. She wears sharp spurs on her heels, which could metaphorically suggest how she treats men as well as her horse. All these uncertainties and ambiguities are richly explored by Chaucer.

Medieval and modern interpretations

Throughout the study of *The Wife of Bath's Prologue* and *Tale* it is essential to keep in mind the fact that medieval audiences would have responded to Chaucer's stories quite differently from a modern reader. In part this is because they would have encountered the stories differently, probably as being read aloud to a group. More importantly, their values and expectations would have been different. Essentially, the whole of Chaucer's audience would have been Catholic. Marriage was one of the basic sacraments, and the medieval Church's teachings were clear. Marriage was for life (the traditional 'till death us do part'), and had to be undertaken devoutly and for the purpose of begetting children. The Wife of Bath, although not definitely outside the letter of the law, was at odds with its spirit. She seems to treat marriage as an opportunity for self-advancement, she is interested in its sexual rather than its procreative aspect, and she welcomes the opportunity to be widowed and re-married.

The audience may well have been amused by the Wife's outrageous and outspoken views, but they would have been in no doubt that she was flouting the morals and attitudes of the established Church.

The audience's response would also have been conditioned by their views about the place and role of women in society. The medieval Christian view

Build critical skills

Comment on the ways in which the Wife is presented in *The General Prologue*. To what extent does the character presented here reflect the one we meet in *The Wife of Bath's Prologue* and *Tale*? Make close references to a range of features.

▲ An image of the Wife of Bath from a fifteenth-century manuscript

▲ Claire Benedict as The Wife of Bath in a Royal Shakespeare Company production of *The Canterbury Tales*

held strongly that women were inferior and subservient to men, in both social and spiritual terms. In this sense the Wife is even more in conflict with the traditional attitudes of her time, because she champions the cause of women and even argues that they should rule over men – a stance that could well be seen as heretical. Again, the audience would have found this entertaining.

Chaucer's original audience would also have had quite different views from contemporary ones about the nature and role of literature. Almost all medieval literature was expected to have a purpose – that is, to be something beyond just entertainment. Most commonly it had a moral or directly religious purpose. Chaucer's tales would be expected to offer moral teaching or guidance, and the Wife of Bath, as a character engaged in a Christian pilgrimage, could be expected to deliver a Christian message. The character herself would be taken more as a type or stereotype; as representative rather than individual.

It is evident that the Wife of Bath herself is not delivering a moral message of a traditional kind – rather the opposite. So Chaucer's audience would be looking at her prologue and tale in terms of the author's intentions, and in this regard it is important to remember that this is just one of several of *The Canterbury Tales* that address the theme of marriage. Chaucer seems to present a whole range of opinions and attitudes, and the Wife of Bath's is one of the most extreme. She does not support the traditional view that the man is dominant; she does not even argue for equality between man and wife. For her, nothing less than female dominance is acceptable, and both her prologue and her tale carry the same message. Her views would have provoked considerable discussion among Chaucer's audience, but it is hard to conceive that Chaucer anticipated many of them endorsing the Wife's views. The more likely alternative is that many of the audience would have seen her as a representative figure, embodying exactly the kind of vices and faults that so many medieval authorities ascribed to women. The medieval Church blamed Eve for the Fall of Man and was deeply misogynistic; for a woman to claim even equality with men would have been unthinkable.

At the same time, it is highly probable that many of the women in Chaucer's audience would have responded positively to the Wife's comments about male behaviour. They would have enjoyed the comedy of her anecdotes about the way she treated her husbands. Few, however, would have gone so far as to wish for the reversal of male and female roles. The Wife's prologue and tale would certainly have invited discussion about the proper relationships between men and women in marriage, and both male and female listeners may have argued the value of a more equal arrangement, as is found in *The Franklin's Tale*.

A modern audience may approach the text quite differently. For us, literature may be purely entertainment – we do not automatically expect to find a deliberate moral or religious message in what we read. We may enjoy the Wife's prologue and tale as a funny and often accurate observation about the way marriages can work out, and how women can overcome the restrictions that society and religion place upon them.

Taking it further ▶

Consider the representations of the Wife in this guide, then compare them with the modern interpretation of the character in the BBC dramatisation (see the 'Taking it further' section of this guide, p.98). To what extent do you think the BBC version successfully captures Chaucer's Wife of Bath?

Modern views of characterisation look much more for the portrayal of individual characters and characteristics, and it is no surprise that the Wife is one of the most popular of Chaucer's creations. She seems to be fully developed as a character, so that we feel we know her like a real person, with all her idiosyncrasies and mannerisms. The modern mind is taught to value the uniqueness of the individual, and the Wife of Bath can easily be understood in this way. This approach is beguiling, but it is a product of a culture that has gone through the development of psychological realism in the twentieth century.

Equally, our view of the place of women in Western society has changed considerably since Chaucer's time, and indeed within the last 50 years. It is easy to see the Wife as a proto-feminist, correctly challenging all the entrenched doctrines and attitudes of her time and championing the rights of women. Again, this is an attractive interpretation for a culture that has experienced the shift in attitudes and beliefs that have marked the last two centuries and more.

These different interpretations mean that we may emerge with different understandings of Chaucer's intentions. We may see him as an enlightened and progressive author, challenging all the preconceptions of his age and encouraging radical opinions. That is one of the reasons why Chaucer is the best known and most popular medieval English writer, because – like Shakespeare – he seems to be as topical in our age as in his own. The differences between likely medieval and modern responses underlie much of the work that you will undertake on *The Wife of Bath's Prologue* and *Tale*. Remember that there are no clear-cut or 'correct' answers. The willingness to express alternatives or uncertainties is a key aspect of an A-level answer.

> **TASK**
> Write down your own response to the Wife early in your study of the text, and again at a later stage when you have much more detailed knowledge. Has your reaction to her changed? Has your opinion of her become more settled, or more ambivalent? Try to discuss this at various times with fellow students and your teachers.

Other characters

The other characters in *The Wife of Bath's Prologue* and *Tale* may be briefly dealt with, because they are not 'characters' as one might find in more modern, 'realistic' fiction. Instead they are functional, serving specific purposes according to Chaucer's (and the Wife's) intentions.

In the prologue

The first three husbands

These husbands are not differentiated or individualised at all. The Wife lumps them together as 'goode men, and riche, and olde' (line 197), the latter two being the reasons she marries them. She could dominate and outwit them, and she delights in emphasising their sexual impotence: 'unnethe mighte they the statut holde' (line 204). They can offer no resistance or threat to her. Note that the word 'goode' is itself sarcastic; their goodness consists only of the fact that they are rich and likely to die soon.

Her fourth husband

The fourth husband represents resistance to the Wife's will, as he was 'a revelour' and had 'a paramour'. He could not dominate her, however, and she 'in his owene grece … made him frie', 'for verray jalousie' (lines 486–87). He receives no extended treatment in the prologue and we do not hear his voice. The Wife's callous dismissal of him in line 500, 'it nis but wast to burye him preciously', underlines her contempt.

Jankin

Although Jankin is the only named character apart from the Wife, and even though he forms the subject of a large section of her prologue (lines 503–828), he too is more a stereotype than an individual. There is a traditional representation of the middle-aged woman falling for a young man (she is 40 when they marry; he is 20), 'which that I took for love, and no richesse' (line 526). This gives him power over her, which he exploits with his misogynistic behaviour. He is the representation of medieval misogyny specifically because he possesses a book in which are bound all the major anti-feminist writings of the period, and which 'for his desport he wolde rede alway' (line 670). He thus tries to assert dominance over his wife. This culminates in their fight: he retaliates against her assault, 'and with his fest he smoot me on the heed' (line 795). This is his last act of resistance and he is comically subservient thereafter: 'he yaf me al the bridel in myn hond' (line 813).

In the tale

None of the characters in the tale is named, which immediately indicates that it is their function that matters, not their individuality.

The knight

The knight simply represents traditional male power and domination over women, which will be reversed by the end of the tale. After his initial act of rape, he becomes subservient to female characters, first 'the queene and othere ladies' of Arthur's court, then the hag, who is the only person who can save him.

The hag

This supernatural figure, with the power to transform herself into a beautiful woman at the end, is partially an image of the Wife of Bath herself, but more generally the representation of the dominant woman who can behave better than men and who has absolute power over their fate and their behaviour. She is not a consistent character. She is a counterpart for the Wife in her amused contempt for men, best seen when she criticises her husband's behaviour on their wedding night (lines 1086–95), but she is also a mouthpiece for Chaucer in her long sermon on the virtues of 'gentillesse' (lines 1104–218), which is discussed in the 'Summaries and commentaries' section, page 15 of this guide.

Arthur's court

It is consonant with the whole of *The Wife of Bath's Prologue* and *Tale* that King Arthur himself should submit to the will of his wife and her ladies. Neither he nor they are characterised other than this.

Writer's methods: Form, structure and language

Target your thinking

- How has Chaucer used the narrator's voice to shape your responses as the text unfolds? (**AO1**)
- How does Chaucer use iambic pentameter and rhyme in *The Wife of Bath's Prologue* and *Tale*? (**AO2**)
- How does Chaucer's use of humour create different possibilities for interpretation of the text? (**AO5**)

Form

The Wife of Bath's Tale is a poetic narrative written in rhyming couplets of iambic pentameter, narrated by the Wife of Bath, one of the pilgrim characters in *The Canterbury Tales*. It is preceded by a prologue, in the same poetic form, where the Wife talks about her personal experiences of marriage.

You are in an unusual position when studying *The Wife of Bath's Prologue* and *Tale* for examination purposes, because the text is set in isolation. It forms a tiny part of a much larger whole, *The Canterbury Tales*, and you cannot hope to understand *The Wife of Bath's Prologue* and *Tale* without a clear sense of this immediate context. *The Wife of Bath's Tale* is one story in a large collection of stories (Chaucer originally intended there to be 120 of them, of which he wrote 24). There is plenty of material in this guide to help you, but you should aim to look at a copy of the complete *Canterbury Tales* in order to get a sense of its size and purpose. You will immediately discover that *The Wife of Bath's Prologue* and *Tale* is unusual within the context of *The Canterbury Tales*: whereas most of the tales in the collection have no or only a short introduction, in the case of the Wife of Bath the prologue is twice the length of the story that follows it. The only comparable example is *The Pardoner's Prologue*, but even he takes only 100 lines to introduce himself.

Taking it further ▶

Study one of the modernised versions of *The Canterbury Tales* in order to see the variety of tales in the collection and how *The Wife of Bath's Prologue* and *Tale* fits into it.

Sources and analogues

The Wife of Bath's Prologue

There is no direct source for *The Wife of Bath's Prologue*, and for many people it is one of the marks of Chaucer's true originality. Chaucer blends a narrative confessional style with a wealth of allusion and quotation from literature, demonstrating the extent of his knowledge and scholarship. He places all this learning in the mouth of a character as unlike himself as possible: the Wife is coarse, self-obsessed and often ill-informed. The main sources of material are the Bible and the anti-feminist writings of a number of authors, particularly St Jerome, Theophrastus and Walter Map. Authors from both Classical and more modern periods are cited. The character of the Wife herself is partly based on the figure of La Vieille (the Old Woman) in the French work *Roman de la Rose*, which Chaucer knew well and which he partly translated into English.

St Jerome

St Jerome (c.345–420) was one of the great early Christian scholars, who translated the Bible into Latin and wrote a large number of theological works. The one used freely by Chaucer is the *Epistola adversus Jovinianum* (*Letter against Jovinianus*). St Jerome preached and practised a life of extreme asceticism – the denial of bodily pleasures in order to enhance holiness. Women were therefore seen as a temptation to sin.

Theophrastus

Theophrastus (c.370–c.288BC) was a Greek writer and philosopher. His *Liber aureolous de nuptiis* (*Golden Book of Marriage*) is quoted in full by St Jerome and contains much misogynistic material, which Chaucer adapts for his purposes.

Walter Map

Walter Map (1140–c.1210) was an Anglo-Welsh writer who rose to become Archdeacon of Oxford. His *Epistola Valerii* (*Letter of Valerius*) is a satirical work condemning marriage.

La Vieille

The *Roman de la Rose* is a 20,000-line thirteenth-century allegorical poem. One of its characters, La Vieille (the Old Woman), is a retired prostitute who talks about how to outwit men. She, like the Wife of Bath, delivers a monologue in which she looks back on her own life and justifies her behaviour. Both the style and the substance of her speeches suggest that she was a source from which Chaucer derived ideas in creating the Wife of Bath.

The Wife of Bath's Tale

Medieval literature did not prize originality and Chaucer, like Shakespeare, freely borrowed from material available to him. The source for *The Wife of Bath's Tale* is most likely to have been a folktale, transmitted orally and no longer known to us. The figure of the bewitched 'loathly lady' is a common one. The basic story seems to have been popular and appears through the ages in a number of guises. Of particular interest are the versions that are analogous to Chaucer's tale.

The three most direct analogues of *The Wife of Bath's Tale* are: *The Tale of Florent* by Chaucer's friend John Gower, in Book 1 of his long story collection *Confessio Amantis*; the anonymous *The Wedding of Sir Gawain and Dame*

> **Context**
>
> You should make it your business to become familiar with at least some of the contextual material mentioned in this guide. This will give you a much better sense of the way medieval literature works, with its constant reliance on authorities and references.

Ragnelle; and the ballad *The Marriage of Sir Gawain*. *The Tale of Florent* is contemporary with *The Wife of Bath's Prologue* and *Tale*; the other two are known from only much later manuscripts.

Unreliable narrator

You should read this in conjunction with the 'Contexts' section, 'The multiple narrators of *The Canterbury Tales*', on page 63 of this guide.

The immediate form of *The Wife of Bath's Prologue* and *Tale* features a common device in the shape of the 'unreliable narrator'; that is to say, a narrator whose personal and partial viewpoint means that the audience cannot accept anything she says on trust, unlike a conventional novel where the 'omniscient narrator' truthfully directs what the reader needs to know. Because of the layers of narrative taking place, your response to *The Wife of Bath's Prologue* and *Tale* must be a complex one. The Wife of Bath is one of Chaucer's most vivid creations, so this makes multiple narrations a key issue when studying her prologue and tale. In every line you need to look behind the character of the Wife to consider what effect Chaucer the author is trying to achieve. In the case of *The Wife of Bath's Prologue* and *Tale* you need not concern yourself with the persona of Chaucer as a pilgrim narrator – he is not 'visible'. The issue is deciding how far Chaucer as an author endorses the Wife's views, or conversely how far he is using her to represent views that are at variance with his own.

In many ways this is the single most important question in defining your response to *The Wife of Bath's Prologue* and *Tale*, but it is dependent on a view of *The Canterbury Tales* beyond the immediate confines of the Wife of Bath's section. This is where studying the Wife in isolation is limiting and why resulting judgements need to be made with caution. Your response is an entirely personal matter, but it will depend on the preconceptions you bring to the study of Chaucer, the breadth of your knowledge of *The Canterbury Tales* and its background in order to put the Wife's contribution in context, and the depth of your understanding of *The Wife of Bath's Prologue* and *Tale* itself.

The one safe thing that may be said is that no simplistic answer will do. It is not true that the Wife of Bath is an embodiment of medieval vice, any more than that she is a fully realised individual character railing at the inadequacies of men. It is through extended study, discussion and thought that you will be able to develop the informed judgement required for A-level. A single example will suffice to show the kind of consideration that needs to be given to the text throughout:

> For trusteth wel, it is an impossible
> That any clerk wol speke good of wives,
> But if it be of hooly seintes lives,
> Ne of noon oother womman never the mo.

(lines 688–91)

Taking it further ▶

These analogues are summarised in the 'Contexts' section, on page 67 of this guide. Examine the original texts via the internet.

Build critical skills

What is the effect of the triple negative in line 691, 'Ne of noon oother womman never the mo'?

◁ **Top ten quotation**

Who is being laughed at here? A sophisticated response is required. The audience may laugh *with* the Wife of Bath and share her awareness that nearly all medieval literature is written by religious men and is anti-feminist. They may laugh *at* the Wife of Bath, if they believe Chaucer is presenting her as exactly the kind of wicked woman that the literature condemns, confirming its truthfulness. Or they may laugh at Chaucer, who is after all yet another man painting a picture of female behaviour in the way that he chooses. *The Canterbury Tales* is emphatically not by a woman writer. The balance of judgement will also depend on whether the medieval context is being considered, or whether the reader is looking at it from a modern perspective.

Structure

The imbalance between prologue and tale means that *The Wife of Bath's Prologue* and *Tale* is unique. You need constantly to take into account the relationship between prologue and tale, recognising that in some ways the tale is a kind of *exemplum* that the Wife uses to reinforce her message. You also need to be aware of two immediate contexts. First, the Wife is speaking to the other pilgrims on the journey, so her contribution is part of a larger discussion among them, particularly about the nature of marriage; second, Chaucer himself has placed the narrative as part of a much wider examination of important themes, of which marriage is just one.

▲ Pilgrims on the road to Canterbury, from a sixteenth-century mural: North Reading Room, west wall, Library of Congress John Adams Building, Washington, D.C.

At first glance the Wife's prologue seems unstructured and rambling, just as if a real person were speaking and sharing her thoughts. This is, of course, an illusion created by the author. The prologue can be broken down into a carefully crafted series of sections; these are the partitions used in the 'Summaries and commentaries' section of the guide (see p.3). They are listed here because it is vitally important that you clarify the structure of the prologue in your own mind, otherwise it can seem like an amorphous and rather daunting mass.

- Lines 1–162: the Wife's views on marriage.
- Lines 163–93: the Pardoner's interruption.
- Lines 194–451: her first three husbands.
- Lines 452–502: her fourth husband.
- Lines 503–626: her courtship with Jankin.
- Lines 627–828: Jankin, her fifth husband.
- Lines 829–56: the Friar and the Summoner.

As can be seen, the Wife's prologue starts with her views on the nature of marriage, and is then built around her successive accounts of her five husbands, culminating in the extended treatment of the last of them, Jankin. The brief interruptions by other pilgrims serve to emphasise the nature of the text and to remind the audience that they are listening to a dramatic monologue. The Pardoner and the Friar interrupt her through exasperation, and represent what the audience themselves might wish to say.

The Wife of Bath's Tale has an altogether crisper and tighter structure, as might be expected. The Wife has changed from personal reminiscence to being the more conventional narrator of a traditional story.

- Lines 857–81: the introduction.
- Lines 882–88: the knight rapes a young woman.
- Lines 889–918: the knight's challenge.
- Lines 919–88: his search for an answer.
- Lines 989–1013: he meets the old hag.
- Lines 1014–45: the knight's answer.
- Lines 1046–103: the marriage.
- Lines 1104–218: 'Gentillesse'.
- Lines 1219–64: the resolution.

There is a clear narrative line here. The introduction sets the story firmly within the ambit of Arthurian literature – 'In th'olde dayes of the King Arthour' (line 857) – so we are expecting a courtly tale of knightly endeavour. The Wife instantly breaks this expectation by making the knight guilty of rape, the most damning instance of male domination: 'By verray force, he rafte hire maidenhed' (line 888). The story then follows his condemnation, the challenge he is set, and how he fulfils it. There is even a twist at the end, as in many stories, where the hag reveals herself to be a beautiful woman. The only surprise for the modern reader is the significant intrusion into the narrative of the 100-line digression on 'gentillesse', which takes up a quarter of the tale. Although this may seem strange to us, it would have been commonplace for a medieval audience, who would expect to hear such moral 'sermoning' in almost every story.

It is important that you hold in mind the parallels between the prologue and the tale, as well as understanding the separate structure of each. The whole of

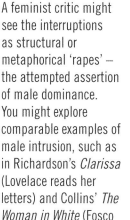

TASK

Look closely at the interruptions by the Pardoner and the Friar. How do they help to break up the Wife's monologue and allow Chaucer to give it clearer organisation?

Taking it further ▶

A feminist critic might see the interruptions as structural or metaphorical 'rapes' – the attempted assertion of male dominance. You might explore comparable examples of male intrusion, such as in Richardson's *Clarissa* (Lovelace reads her letters) and Collins' *The Woman in White* (Fosco reads and writes in Marian's diary).

the prologue is designed by the Wife to demonstrate her assertion that women should be dominant over men. Her tale, therefore, acts as a practical example, or *exemplum*, of this process in action: a resolution is only achieved when the knight submits completely to the will of the hag. Chaucer carefully creates linguistic parallels between the end of the prologue and the end of the tale to show the unity of the two – you should examine and compare lines 813–25 of the prologue and lines 1230–48 of the tale. In an important sense, you can treat *The Wife of Bath's Prologue* and *Tale* as a single text with a bipartite structure.

Language

Chaucer's verse

The metre that Chaucer adopted for most of *The Canterbury Tales* became the standard one used in English poetry for the next five hundred years, and in this sense at least he should be familiar to the modern reader. He writes in iambic pentameter, the metre used by Shakespeare, Milton, Keats and all of the great poets prior to the twentieth century. The lines are arranged into pairs called heroic couplets, a grand style often undermined by its content.

'Iambic' refers to the rhythm of the verse: a repeated pattern of two syllables, with the first syllable unstressed and the second syllable stressed, as in words like 'remind' and 'believe'. An iamb is one of these two-syllable, unstressed/ stressed patterns. Each pair of syllables is called a foot. 'Pentameter' (literally five measures or 'feet') means that five feet are joined together, to make a ten-syllable (decasyllabic) regular line: da dum da dum da dum da dum da dum. The conventional mark for a stressed syllable is /, and the mark for an unstressed syllable is ~. A couplet of iambic pentameter therefore goes like this:

> Bifil that in that seson on a day,
>
> ~ / ~ / ~ / ~ / ~ /
>
> In Southwerk at the Tabard as I lay
>
> ~ / ~ / ~ / ~ / ~ /

> (*The General Prologue*, lines 19–20)

The reason that this became the staple metre of English poetry is because iambic rhythm is closest to natural speech – whenever you speak a sentence, it contains more iambs than any other rhythm. Chaucer shows astonishing assurance and versatility in handling the iambic form. He can use it for formal description in a stately manner:

> In th'olde dayes of the King Arthour,
> Of which that Britons speken greet honour,
> Al was this land fulfild of faierie.

> (lines 857–59)

He can use it for fast-paced action:

> Al sodeynly thre leves have I plight
> Out of his book, right as he radde, and eke
> I with my fest so took him on the cheke
> That in oure fyr he fil bakward adoun.

(lines 790–93)

He uses it for rhetorical effect:

> Poverte is this, although it seme alenge…
> Poverte ful ofte, whan a man is lowe…
> Poverte a spectacle is, as thinketh me…

(lines 1199, 1201, 1203)

But most frequently, and most effectively, he uses it to represent speech:

> O Lord! the peyne I dide hem and the wo,
> Ful giltelees, by Goddes sweete pine!

(lines 384–85)

> Wy, taak it al! lo, have it every deel!
> Peter! I shrewe yow, but ye love it weel.

(lines 445–46)

In his earlier work, Chaucer frequently used an octosyllabic (eight-syllable) line, which was common at the time; the use of iambic pentameter marks his maturity as a poet.

Chaucer's language

There is no doubt that the Middle English of *The Canterbury Tales* comes between the modern reader and an easy appreciation of the work. After a little practice, however, most of the difficulties presented by the language drop away. The vocabulary can present problems because, while some words look familiar or obvious, they are not. For example, the word 'wood' can mean wood but, in a different context, means mad, as in the description of the lion in *The Wife of Bath's Prologue* (line 429). The solution is to keep a careful eye on the notes and glossary of your edition.

The easiest way to start to understand Chaucer's language is to read it aloud, or to listen to it being read. Chaucer intended his verse to be spoken, and it makes more sense when it is. Remember the following:

- Most letters are pronounced, so that 'knight' sounds like 'cnicht' and 'mighte' like 'micht'.
- The final 'e' on words like 'fooles' is normally pronounced ('fool-es'), unless it is followed by another vowel.

Build critical skills

How does alliteration help to create emphasis in this passage?

TASK

Find your own examples of different ways in which Chaucer uses the verse form; keep this collection together so that you can refer to it and use appropriate examples in your essays.

- ◥ Some vowels have different sound values, but do not worry about this initially.
- ◥ Words imported from French would still sound French, so 'dotage' would be 'dotarge' and 'mariage' would be 'mar-ee-arge'.

With these few simple adjustments, aim to read the verse as if it were ordinary conversation. Try to ignore the rhythm and rhyme – they will take care of themselves. Your edition should have further detail on aspects of pronunciation, but the primary objective is to get a sense of the flow of the language.

Modernisations

Another good way of gaining confidence in reading the language is to create a Modern English version of each line. This can be done aloud in class, or you can jot down a literal version as you go along, for example:

Top ten quotation

Experience, though noon auctoritee Were in this world, is right ynogh for me (lines 1–2)	Experience, even if no authority Existed in this world, is quite sufficient for me

It does not take long before Chaucer's English becomes almost as straightforward as Shakespeare's. You never quite lose your caution in looking at it (as you should not with Shakespeare), but you do become more comfortable working with it.

It may be a good idea to obtain a modern version of *The Wife of Bath's Prologue* and *Tale*, and even of the whole of *The Canterbury Tales*. This will allow you to check your own rendering of each line, so that you are confident you have the correct basic meaning.

The Wife's use of language

The Wife of Bath has a distinctive voice, making her one of the most memorable figures in literature. She is fast-talking, breezy and chatty, like somebody you meet in a pub who insists on telling you their life story. This is an exact analogy, because this is the premise of *The Wife of Bath's Prologue* and *Tale*; she is ostensibly riding along telling her life story to a group of strangers whom she met in the inn in Southwark. Her language in the prologue is colloquial; Chaucer is deliberately creating the illusion of an ordinary woman speaking conversationally, despite the rhyming couplet form. In this he is similar to and often compared with Shakespeare, whose plays are also largely written in iambic pentameter. The nature of the language in the tale, though, tends to be more formal, as one might expect in a narrated story.

Chaucer makes an enormous effort to make the Wife's speech as naturalistic as possible, which is one of the reasons why modern readers and critics find it so easy to treat her as if she were a realistic character.

Much of the Wife's discourse is built of conversational and colloquial elements. You will find many examples for yourself during your study of the text; the following are designed to illustrate the range of effects that Chaucer achieves.

▲ The pilgrims travel to Canterbury

Conversational style

There are numerous examples of her conversational and colloquial style, many of them showing her addressing her imaginary audience directly:

> Lo, heere... *(line 35)*
> I pray yow, telleth me. *(line 61)*
> Ye knowe... *(line 90)*
> But that I praye to al this compaignie... *(line 189)*

She uses many rhetorical questions:

> Why sholde men thanne speke of it vileynie? *(line 34)*
> ...where comanded he virginitee? *(line 62)*

She evens forgets what she was saying:

> But now, sire, lat me se, what I shal seyn?
> A ha! by God, I have my tale ageyn.
>
> (lines 585–86)

43

Chaucer also adds to the verisimilitude by having her frequently report her own conversations with her husbands, and by having interruptions to her discourse from the Pardoner and the Friar.

Colloquial words and phrases

Alongside her quoting of 'auctoritees', the Wife uses a wealth of homely phrases and examples:

> Whoso that first to mille comth, first grint; *(line 389)*
> With empty hand men may none haukes lure. *(line 415)*
> The flour is goon, ther is namoore to telle. *(line 477)*
> ...nat worth a leek. *(line 572)*
> ...I hadde alwey a coltes tooth. *(line 602)*

She frequently uses informal or vulgar vocabulary, such as 'kaynard' (line 235), 'queynte' (line 332), 'bele chose' (euphemism, line 510), 'pissed' (line 534). She also uses oaths, such as 'benedicitee!' (line 280) and 'God have hir soule!' (line 530).

Conversational sentence structures

> As evere moote I drinken wyn or ale,
> I shal seye sooth, tho housbondes that I hadde,
> As thre of hem were goode, and two were badde.
>
> (lines 194–96)

> But now to purpos, why I tolde thee
> That I was beten for a book, pardee!
>
> (lines 711–12)

Against these are set the more formal aspects of her speech, particularly her use of rhetorical devices. Chaucer grants to the Wife a passing acquaintance with rhetorical techniques, which were developed systematically in the Middle Ages by writers such as Geoffrey of Vinsauf. It is not necessary for you to use the Classical terms, such as *occupatio*, *amplificatio* and *abbreviatio*, but you should be able to recognise and describe such features.

Rhetoric

Rhetorical questions are instantly visible:

> How manye mighte she have in mariage?
>
> (line 23)

The opening of the prologue reveals a familiar politician's trick (an example of *occupatio*), where the Wife claims that she does not need 'auctoritee' – and then spends the next 150 lines citing the Bible.

The whole of her prologue can be seen as *amplificatio*, the gradual accretion of material to add emphasis and force to an idea. In her case it reaches absurd lengths, prompting the Friar's tart and contrasting use of *abbreviatio* (the shortening of an idea to make an emphatic point) at the end:

> This is a long preamble of a tale!
>
> (line 831)

Formal vocabulary

The Wife is perfectly capable of using formal and even technical terms, such as 'auctoritee' (line 1), 'bigamie' (line 33), 'visitaciouns' (line 555).

Formal sentence structures

When the Wife is formal, her sentence structures become more formal too:

> Another Romain tolde he me by name,
>
> That, for his wyf was at a someres game
>
> Withouten his witing, he forsook hire eke.
>
> (lines 647–49)

Chaucer's achievement is to seamlessly blend the informal and formal aspects of her discourse to give us an illusion of unity. If we view the matter in a detached way, it is hard to reconcile the Wife's coarse and colloquial speech with the sophistication of her supposed learning and control of narrative. Chaucer, however, involves the audience so completely from the first line that we do not notice this tension.

When we turn to her tale, the formal nature of her discourse is immediately evident at the opening, where she uses a traditional story-telling mode, the once-upon-a-time style familiar to us from fairy stories:

> In th'olde dayes of the King Arthour,
>
> Of which that Britons speken greet honour,
>
> Al was this land fulfild of faierie.
>
> (lines 857–59)

Chaucer, though, is careful to litter the tale with the kind of informal speech and effects that characterise the prologue, in order to maintain the Wife's narrative voice. It is vital that the tale does not seem disconnected, as the cumulative weight of the Wife's argument depends on her prologue and tale being taken together. Hence her own apparent interruptions into her narrative:

> But that tale is nat worth a rake-stele.
>
> Pardee, we wommen konne no thing hele;
>
> Witnesse on Mida, – wol ye heere the tale?
>
> (lines 949–51)

Taking it further ▶

Explore the importance of rhetoric in the Middle Ages and look at some of the devices used by Chaucer and other writers. A website such as the Forest of Rhetoric at http://humanities. byu.edu/rhetoric/silva. htm is invaluable here, and will give an insight into a subject that was one of the seven Liberal Arts taught in medieval universities, although it receives little or no emphasis in modern education.

Context

The use of the Classical story of Midas, from Ovid's *Metamorphoses*, is a typical example of the way medieval authors freely mixed their source material. The Classical story is here used in the middle of an Arthurian tale.

This intrusion, with the wonderfully homely term 'rake-stele' to emphasise that this is the same voice as in her prologue, leads to a 30-line digression into the tale of Midas before she returns to her tale. The narrative effect is similar to that of her prologue, where she often seems to change direction before returning to her central theme.

Even the loathly lady whom the knight marries is given the kind of colloquial manner that invites the reader to identify her with the Wife:

> Swich arrogance is nat worth an hen.

(line 1112)

Generally speaking, however, much of the tale operates in formal story-telling mode. Overall, Chaucer skilfully blends the formal and informal to give us the impression that *The Wife of Bath's Prologue* and *Tale* is a unified work.

Exempla

The most noticeably formal and rhetorical aspect of the Wife's prologue is the way she uses lists of examples to support her case. This may seem unusual to modern eyes, but was commonplace in medieval literature, where authorities counted for so much. The most striking instance is in lines 711–87, where she is recounting what was in the book that Jankin read to her. She cites no fewer than ten individual examples from biblical and Classical sources, followed by a more general list of women's vices.

Humour

The mode of *The Canterbury Tales* is comedy. Whatever our final judgements about the Wife of Bath, and about Chaucer's purpose in writing, it is the humour of the tales that is most instantly striking. Chaucer uses a wide variety of comic techniques to make his stories entertaining, and you will need to have your own lists of examples of humour in order to deal with the topic. The following are examples of the main types of humour in *The Wife of Bath's Prologue* and *Tale*.

Situational humour

The Wife's behaviour at her fourth husband's funeral: In lines 593–602 of the prologue, the Wife's fourth husband is being buried, but even at this supposedly solemn moment she is lasciviously staring at Jankin's legs: 'me thoughte he hadde a paire / of legges and of feet so clene and faire' (lines 597–98). The comedy is compounded by her admission that she is a 40-year-old woman eyeing up a man half her age.

The knight's wedding night: In lines 1083–105 of the tale, the knight takes his wife to bed on their wedding night. The humour lies in the contrast between the knight's squirming reluctance to touch her, and her blithe manner and feigned surprise. He 'walweth and he turneth to and fro' (line 1085), while she 'lay smilinge everemo' (line 1086). When she rebukes him for his churlish behaviour,

Build critical skills

Why does Chaucer use the present tense for 'walweth' and 'turneth' in line 1085?

he cannot resist protesting that 'Thou art so loothly, and so oold also'. Even without the remainder of the tale, the audience might think he is being justly punished for his original crime of rape.

Stereotyping

The hen-pecked husband: The whole prologue revolves around the traditional motif of the nagging wife and the hen-pecked husband, a rich source of comedy throughout the ages. This is particularly evident in lines 235–378, where the Wife treats the pilgrims to a 150-line account of the kind of incessant verbal assault that she used on her first husbands. This is comic in itself; in relating it, the Wife reveals herself to be exactly the stereotype of a nagging wife that the hen-pecked husband traditionally dreads. The audience is meant to laugh at the poor husbands, but can also laugh at the wife. Even before this, the Pardoner has been so appalled by her antics that he declares himself lucky to have escaped:

> I was aboute to wedde a wyf; allas,
> What sholde I bye it on my flessh so deere?

> (lines 166–67)

There is further comedy here when it is remembered that the Pardoner is a eunuch.

Satire

Satire – holding up folly or vice for ridicule – is a major aim in many of *The Canterbury Tales*, and Chaucer frequently uses it to attack more than one target.

The Wife of Bath: Certainly the Wife herself is ridiculous, from the exaggerated portrait presented in *The General Prologue* to the grossly extended prologue that Chaucer permits her before she begins her tale. Her outspoken manner and uncompromising attitude are obvious targets for Chaucer and the pilgrims to laugh at. In this reading, the whole of her attack on men is seen to be self-defeating, because she embodies all the vices for which women have traditionally been condemned. Even her name is ironic, as Alison means 'noble' – the Wife is noble neither by birth nor by character.

Men: She in turn ridicules much of male behaviour, and nobody in either her prologue or her tale emerges with much credit. Your view of exactly where the main targets of satire lie will depend on your overall reading, which should be developed through the study of the whole text.

Bawdiness

The use of crude language: Chaucer, like Giovanni Boccaccio, is partly famous as a bawdy writer, most strikingly in *The Miller's Tale*. Although bawdy is in fact a tiny element of *The Canterbury Tales* as a whole, it adds a distinctive note in certain places. Indeed, such is modern sensitivity that *The Wife of Bath's Prologue* and *Tale* has sometimes been published in expurgated versions. The open use of words like 'queynte' (lines 332 and 444) would probably have been

Taking it further ▶

Satire is the key to the whole of *The Canterbury Tales*, and it is essential that you have a clear understanding of the meaning of the term and the way it is used by Chaucer, and other writers. Start with a good dictionary of literary critical terms, and be prepared to explore how satire is used in texts that you know.

shocking even to a medieval audience; euphemisms like 'bele chose' (lines 447 and 510) and 'quoniam' (line 608) are still brazen. Similarly, the references to 'chambre of Venus' (line 618) and 'privee place' (line 620) confirm the Wife's earthy and unrestrained nature. Chaucer would have included this kind of language to show the contrast between her and the more well-bred and well-spoken pilgrims.

Her treatment of her husbands: Her sexual voraciousness makes her hapless husbands seem laughable:

> I sette hem so a-werke, by my fey,
> That many a night they songen 'weilawey!'
>
> (lines 215–16)

Irony

If satire is one of Chaucer's main purposes, irony is consistently his main weapon, and you should constantly be on the lookout for where the surface meaning of a passage is at odds with the underlying intent. The following are given as examples.

> Deceite, weping, spinning God hath yive
> To wommen kindely, whil that they may live.
>
> (lines 401–02)

Top ten quotation

This seemingly proverbial anti-feminist belief is ironically quoted here by the Wife with approval – she is proud of her deceitfulness. There is also a pun in line 402, where 'kindely' can mean both 'in their nature' and 'kindly'.

> And al was fals, but that I took witnesse
> On Janekin, and on my nece also.
>
> (lines 382–83)

The apparently independent witnesses she calls to confirm her husbands' unreasonable behaviour are in fact her associates and confidantes. She presumably already has an understanding with Jankin, who will eventually become her fifth husband; her relative is one of the women to whom she betrays all her husbands' secrets, as she later confirms in lines 537–38.

> But afterward repented me ful soore;
> He nolde suffre nothing of my list.
>
> (lines 632–33)

The irony here is that Jankin is the one person she has ever truly loved, but it transpires that when they are married he is the most anti-feminist of all her husbands, and even has a book full of writings about the wickedness of women. It is an additional irony that she is guilty of all the faults he details. She is led to say 'I hate him that my vices telleth me' (line 662), despite the fact that she married Jankin for love.

TASK

Find your own examples of the types of humour in the text, and prepare quotations that you can use in your essays.

Contexts

Target your thinking

- How can setting *The Wife of Bath's Prologue* and *Tale* within a broad range of contexts deepen your understanding of the text and the ways in which different readers might respond to it? (**AO3**, **AO5**)
- What links might be traced between *The Wife of Bath's Prologue* and *Tale* and various other literary texts? (**AO4**)

Biographical context

Although nothing is known about Chaucer as a person and almost nothing about his private life, he was a prominent figure in the second half of the fourteenth century, with associations and positions at court. He served under three kings, and was entrusted by Edward III with foreign journeys to handle the king's secret affairs. The public aspects of his life are therefore well documented, and demonstrate that he would have had direct experience of nearly all the kinds of people he represents in *The Canterbury Tales*.

There are some uncertainties and some periods of Chaucer's life for which little is known, but the salient dates are outlined below. The approximate dates for the composition of his literary works are also given.

Key dates and works

c.1340–45	Geoffrey Chaucer born, son of a London wine merchant.
1357	Becomes a page in the household of the Countess of Ulster.
1360	Captured while serving in France; ransomed by Edward III.
1366	Journeys to Spain; marries Philippa Rouet around this time.
1367	Appointed Yeoman of the Chamber in the king's household.
1367–77	Journeys abroad on the king's business.
1369	Campaigns in France; appointed Esquire in the king's household.
Pre-1372	*The Book of the Duchess.*
1372–73	First journey to Italy.
1372–80	*The House of Fame.*
1374	Appointed Comptroller of Customs and Subsidy.
1377	Edward III dies; accession of Richard II.
1378	Second journey to Italy.
1380–86	*The Parliament of Fowls*; *Troilus and Criseyde*; *The Legend of Good Women.*

▲ Geoffrey Chaucer

Taking it further ▷

Explore Chaucer's life in more detail and consider how far his worldview as expressed in *The Canterbury Tales* was affected by his background and experiences.

1385	Appointed Justice of the Peace for Kent.
1385–1400	*The Canterbury Tales*.
1386	Sits in Parliament as Knight of the Shire for Kent.
1389	Appointed Clerk to the King's Works.
1391	Appointed Subforester.
1394	Awarded extra grant for good service.
1399	Richard II deposed; accession of Henry IV.
	Previous grants confirmed by Henry IV.
1400	Dies on 25 October; buried in Westminster Abbey.

Social context

The three estates model

Medieval society comprised three classes, or estates: those who prayed, those who fought, and those who laboured to sustain the first two groups. In principle, this was the basis of feudal society.

The first estate was the clergy, a large group that maintained the fabric of society through the service of God and the regulation of human affairs. The second estate was the nobility, who were few in number, and were landowners and professional soldiers. The third estate was the vast bulk of ordinary people, who were subject to the laws of both the other groups. In a primarily agrarian society, this group comprised mainly peasants who laboured on the land to create the food and wealth by which society was sustained. A person was born into either the second or third estate, and might enter the first (the clergy) through vocation or for a variety of other reasons, including a desire for security or advancement. Otherwise, people were expected to remain in the rank to which God was seen to have allocated them at birth.

In addition to being members of one of the three estates, medieval women were also placed in one of three categories: virgin, wife or widow. They tended to be thought of as inferior in consequence and importance to men.

In practice, the structure of medieval society was not as simple as the three estates model suggests, and by Chaucer's lifetime significant changes had taken place. From the start, there were inequalities in the third estate, which necessarily covered a vast range of occupations. With the passing of time people strove to better their conditions, and by the fourteenth century there were numerous distortions and anomalies within the system. The range of characters in *The Canterbury Tales* illustrates this. The only members of the nobility are the Knight and his son the Squire. The only true peasant is the Ploughman. There are several members of the clergy, but only three women. The remaining pilgrims all occupy a shifting middle ground; they are technically members of the third estate, but to equate the Man of Law – a wealthy, influential professional – with the Miller is clearly absurd. Although class distinctions continue to exist to this day, it is evident that the feudal division into classes had already lost much of its practical significance long before the Middle Ages ended; *The Canterbury Tales* amply shows how there was a blurring of position, wealth and influence in this period.

Historical context

The late fourteenth century was a time of great change, which makes *The Canterbury Tales* a valuable window on to an important period in English history.

The Black Death

The catalyst for change was the outbreak of the plague known as the Black Death. This swept through Europe and devastated England on several occasions in the fourteenth century, most radically in 1348–49, early in Chaucer's life. The exact figures are unknown, but estimates suggest that up to 40 per cent of England's population died. The effects of this were colossal. Before the mid-fourteenth century, the population had been expanding, meaning that labour was plentiful and land use intensive. Afterwards, labour became scarcer and pressures on the land decreased. Thousands of individual jobs and roles were lost. Inevitably, there was suddenly scope for enterprising people from all ranks of society to seek better conditions and better occupations.

Taking it further ▶

To get an idea of the upheaval caused by the outbreaks of plague in medieval England, imagine how modern Britain might change if nearly half the population was suddenly wiped out by disease.

The Peasants' Revolt

Social unrest was a likely outcome of social change, and it is not surprising that the uprising known as the Peasants' Revolt occurred in 1381. This rebellion was primarily triggered by increased taxation, and resulted in a march on the city of London and demands for the eradication of serfdom. The rebellion gained little of immediate consequence, but it offers an important insight into the way that society was changing at a rapid pace. At the time, Chaucer was living above Aldgate, one of the six city gates of London, so he must have had an intimate awareness of the events that took place.

Language

It was during Chaucer's lifetime that English re-emerged as the official language of court and the law, supplanting the Norman French that William the Conqueror had imposed in the eleventh century and paving the way for the dominance of what would become Modern English. This is reflected in Chaucer's choice of English for all his major works; by comparison, his friend John Gower wrote three major works, one in English, one in French and one in Latin.

The Church

Although it remained a paramount power both in politics and in society, the Church was also subject to upheaval at this time. In 1378, one of the years in which Chaucer visited Italy, the Great Schism took place. This was a rift in the Church that resulted in the election of two popes – an unimaginable situation if one considers the hierarchical significance of the pope as the appointed representative of God on Earth. The Italians had elected Urban VI as pope, but the French, supported by their king, Charles V, appointed Clement VII, who set up his throne in Avignon. Like the Peasants' Revolt, the Great Schism led to further questioning of the authority of established powers, and a greater willingness on the part of ordinary people to press their own claims for rights and privileges.

In England the effects of the upheaval in the Church were felt particularly in the work of John Wycliffe (1328–84), a reformer who attacked papal authority and denounced the Great Schism as the 'Antichrist itself'. He argued that every man had the right to examine the Bible for himself, and sponsored the first translation of the Bible into English. He was a major figure in the latter part of the fourteenth century, and his work led to the heretical movement known as Lollardy. It is debatable whether or not Chaucer had Lollard sympathies; certainly his writing, in particular in *The Canterbury Tales*, attacks abuses within the Church in a way with which Wycliffe would have sympathised.

Cultural context

Chaucer's place in the history of English literature

It was John Dryden in the seventeenth century who labelled Chaucer 'the father of English poetry'. The modern reader may share this belief, because Chaucer is the earliest writer to still be widely known. His language is the most accessible, and the most 'modern', of all the medieval authors, and his emphasis on apparently realistic characters and themes seems modern too. He championed the use of the iambic pentameter and the rhyming couplet in much of his work, and this metre became the staple of English verse for the next 500 years.

He was well known both in his own lifetime and after; many writers, including Shakespeare, were influenced by him and used his work as a source. The term 'father of English poetry' thus contains considerable truth, but it is also a distortion and conceals facts of which the student of Chaucer needs to be aware. Chaucer died six hundred years ago, in 1400. *Beowulf*, the earliest known masterpiece in English, was composed around AD700. By that reckoning, Chaucer lived more than halfway through the chronological history of English literature and as such represents part of a continuing tradition rather than being the inventor of a new one.

It is easy to explain both the error contained in the popular view of Chaucer and his pre-eminence. First, there is the matter of language. *Beowulf* was composed in Anglo-Saxon (also known as Old English), and even Chaucer's great contemporaries, such as William Langland and the anonymous author of *Sir Gawain and the Green Knight*, were writing in a style that dated back nearly a thousand years. This was the so-called alliterative style, in which alliteration and a flexible rhythm were used to give lines shape and structure. In contrast,

Chaucer wrote in a new-fangled style influenced by French and Italian, using a set metre (mainly iambic pentameter in *The Canterbury Tales*; see 'Chaucer's verse' on p.40 of this guide) and rhyming couplets. His language was that used in London and, since London was the capital of England, it was inevitable that the language used by Chaucer would be that which came to predominate and therefore be most familiar to subsequent generations. Moreover, until Chaucer's day there had been only a small amount of 'literature', in the sense of material that was written down. In a largely illiterate society, most culture was communicated orally, and written versions (including *Beowulf* itself) are fortuitous historical accidents. Most writing was done in Latin, the language of the educated (which essentially meant monks), and it is only from Chaucer's time onwards that there is a strong tradition of literature written in English.

Other works

Chaucer did not write just *The Canterbury Tales*. His other major work is *Troilus and Criseyde*, a tragic love story based on a supposed incident in the Trojan War. Chaucer borrowed the plot for this from Giovanni Boccaccio, and it was later used by Shakespeare and Dryden. *Troilus and Criseyde* is an 8200-line poem written in a metre known as rhyme royal (a seven-line stanza in iambic pentameter), which Chaucer also used in *The Clerk's Tale* and *The Prioress' Tale*.

Chaucer also wrote a number of short verses, and several long poems of the type known as 'dream visions', in which the narrator falls asleep and dreams the events that the poem relates. His interest in the status and role of women, a noticeable theme in *The Canterbury Tales*, is confirmed by *The Legend of Good Women*, which tells the stories of nine Classical heroines, including Cleopatra and Thisbe.

Chaucer is famed for his wide reading and considerable education, which are illustrated by the fact that a number of his works are translations. He may have translated part of the *Roman de la Rose*, the vast thirteenth-century French poem that is a major source for and influence on Chaucer's own work. He translated from Latin *The Consolation of Philosophy* by Boethius, which was one of the best-known philosophical works in the Middle Ages (although the text dates from the sixth century). Finally, he translated a scientific work, *A Treatise on the Astrolabe* (an instrument for measuring the position of the stars). This demonstrates the breadth of Chaucer's knowledge as well as confirming the interest in astrology that is visible throughout his work, for example in the description of the Doctor of Physic in *The General Prologue* and the detail of Nicholas' learning in *The Miller's Tale*.

Influences

A man as widely read as Chaucer would be familiar with all the great historical writers known in his time, together with many contemporaries. In addition, Chaucer's foreign travels on the king's business would have brought him into direct contact with the works of great European writers such as Boccaccio and

Taking it further ▶

It is important to be aware that Chaucer was a European rather than just an English writer, so it is worth exploring the French and Italian influences on his writing online or in Rowland's *Companion to Chaucer Studies* (see the 'Taking it further' section, on p.97).

Petrarch. Boccaccio's *Decameron* became a direct model for *The Canterbury Tales*. Chaucer was heavily influenced by biblical and religious writings, and by French and Italian writers of his own and previous centuries. It is worth thinking of him as a European rather than as primarily an English writer.

Numerous sources, both general and specific, for and influences on *The Canterbury Tales* have been identified, and you should consult your edition of the text to appreciate the wealth of material on which Chaucer draws.

Contemporaries

Chaucer is the best known of the fourteenth-century writers, but during this period there was a huge flowering of writing in English. This was probably because English was re-emerging as the official language of the country after three centuries of Norman French domination, and also because greater education and literacy allowed the production of true literature, that is work composed in writing rather than orally.

In Chaucer's own lifetime there were two other major English writers whose importance rivals that of Chaucer – William Langland and the Gawain-poet.

William Langland

William Langland wrote the great poem *Piers Plowman*. He was obsessed with the work and wrote three versions of it, ranging from 2500 to 7300 lines, over a period of 30 or 40 years. It is written in the alliterative style, a completely different form of poetry from Chaucer's and one that was a development of Anglo-Saxon verse. *Piers Plowman* is a vast allegorical work in which the eponymous Piers begins as the figure of a humble ploughman (comparable to the Ploughman of *The General Prologue*) and ends up as an allegorical representation of Christ. It is deeply serious, complex and unique.

The Gawain-poet

Meanwhile, perhaps in Cheshire, there was a poet to whom authorship of all four of the poems preserved in the *Pearl* manuscript is usually attributed. The poet's name is not known, but he is most commonly referred to as the Gawain-poet, after his most famous work, *Sir Gawain and the Green Knight*. Like *Piers Plowman*, this poem is written in an alliterative verse form, but its language is now so unfamiliar that it is usually read in a modernised version. It tells the story of a mysterious Green Knight who challenges King Arthur's court to a 'game' at Christmas. He invites someone to chop his head off, but when Gawain does so the Green Knight calmly collects his head and demands the right to return the blow in a year's time. The rest of the poem follows Gawain's dilemmas and tests as he seeks to keep his side of the bargain. The poem is a powerful, complex work that manages to be simultaneously humane, witty, profoundly moral and symbolic.

As well as these two writers there was John Gower, a personal friend of Chaucer's and a major influence on him. Gower's works are no longer held in such esteem, but he is best known for his *Confessio Amantis*.

The existence of these writers points to a vernacular tradition of enormous richness, variety and substance, of which only a small portion has survived into the modern age. As well as Langland, the Gawain-poet and Gower, there was a wealth of material in all forms (poetry, drama and religious prose) that shows that Chaucer was part of a great age of literary output, rather than an isolated and unique genius.

Story collections

In the Middle Ages, storytelling was a common form of communal entertainment. Literacy was scarce, and tales were told and retold, handed down from storyteller to storyteller through generations and centuries. Originally, almost all stories would have been in verse as this made them easier to remember, but as the Middle Ages progressed an increasing number were written in prose. Traditional stories might be gathered together by a scribe, and gradually individual storytellers emerged who adapted material to their own designs and added to it. Collections of stories therefore became common; some were mere agglomerations of tales, while others were unified and written by a single author. A few of these collections are still well known, the most familiar example being *The Thousand and One Nights*.

Contemporary examples

Chaucer would have been influenced by two particular works. The anonymous *Gesta Romanorum* was an amorphous and disparate group of tales, gathered in various forms over a long period but united by a single guiding principle. The tales, many of them traditional or legendary, were viewed as allegories, that is to say literal narratives that could be given a parallel spiritual interpretation. Each tale is followed by an explanation offering a Christian reading of the text. For example, the Classical tale of Atalanta, the swift runner who is beaten by a competitor who throws golden apples to distract her from the race, is seen as an **allegory** of the human soul being tempted by the devil. It is worth considering how far *The Canterbury Tales* can similarly be seen as a diverse group of stories unified by an underlying Christian message. The *Gesta Romanorum* is a vital reminder that medieval literature could be complex, and that medieval audiences expected multiple and concealed meanings in a work of art.

The second work that may be considered an immediate model for Chaucer is the *Decameron* by Giovanni Boccaccio. Chaucer travelled to Italy and may have met Boccaccio; it is certainly true that he knew the Italian poet's work and was probably trying to create an equivalent masterpiece in English. The framework of the *Decameron* is similar to that of *The Canterbury Tales*, in that ten narrators are given the task of telling ten stories each over the course of ten days, making a neat 100 stories in all. Chaucer's scheme has 30 narrators telling four stories

Allegory: an extended metaphor that veils an underlying moral, religious or political meaning.

Taking it further ▷

Look at the *Gesta Romanorum* to see the kind of tradition that lay behind *The Canterbury Tales*. The *Gesta* were frequently translated into English; one version is available on the University of Michigan site (search for *Gesta Romanorum* and follow the http://quod.lib. umich.edu link).

each, making a more substantial total of 120 tales. The fact that this scheme came nowhere near completion, and that Chaucer probably reduced the plan to a single tale for each teller, does not reduce the significance of the comparison.

Chaucer's friend John Gower also produced a story collection, which suggests the popularity of such works in the fourteenth century. Gower's *Confessio Amantis* (*Confession of the Lover*) is a moral work commenting on the seven deadly sins, the same theme as the sermon in *The Parson's Tale*. Gower used some of the same stories as Chaucer, notably the tale of Florent (told by the Wife of Bath) and the tale of Constance (in *The Man of Law's Tale*).

The Canterbury Tales as a story collection

The difference between Chaucer's work and these other story collections is the dynamic link between the tellers and the tales. The *Gesta Romanorum* has no narrator at all; it is simply a collection of separate tales. Although there are ten separate narrators in the *Decameron*, there is no great significance in which narrator tells which tale. In Chaucer's work, the match of tale and teller is frequently a crucial part of the overall meaning. The Knight, the courtliest figure on the pilgrimage, tells a suitably courtly tale. The Miller, the most vulgar of the pilgrims, tells the coarsest story. In the most sophisticated case, the Pardoner, who would be a profitable subject for modern psychoanalysis, introduces his tale by explaining the hypocritical success of his own sales techniques, and then proceeds to attempt to dupe his auditors in exactly the same way. As part of this he tells a devastatingly effective tale of greed and justice, which is integrally linked to both his personality and his practices.

The Canterbury Tales is remarkable because it contains examples of all the kinds of story popular in the medieval period – courtly tales, sermons, saints' lives, **fabliaux**, animal fables – and different verse forms, as well as two tales in prose. This makes *The Canterbury Tales* one of the most diverse of all story collections, and the narrative device of the pilgrimage plays an important part in giving this mix cohesion.

Fabliaux: short medieval tales in rhyme, of a coarsely comic and satirical nature.

It can be difficult to appreciate the significance of Chaucer's overall scheme, both because of the unfinished nature of *The Canterbury Tales* and because A-level students are usually studying one tale in isolation. It is strongly recommended that you become familiar with *The Canterbury Tales* in its entirety, perhaps by reading the whole work in Modern English.

Audience

Chaucer was a courtly writer, composing his works for a courtly and sophisticated audience. In earlier eras, almost all culture would have been oral and communal, with storytellers and poets reciting their works to diverse groups of listeners. The only 'books' were manuscripts that had been copied by hand on to parchment made from animal skins, and these would have been rare and valuable. Almost all manuscripts were of religious texts, and it was not until the later Middle Ages that manuscripts of secular works like Chaucer's became available (more than eighty copies of *The Canterbury Tales* survive). By Chaucer's time, there were sufficient numbers of educated people and manuscript copies to enable private reading parties where one person, for example a lady of the court, would read stories to small groups of friends. An individual might even read stories alone, but that would necessitate the availability of a manuscript and the leisure to peruse it.

▲ One of the surviving copies of *The Canterbury Tales*

Taking it further ▶▷

Listen to the Chaucer text being read aloud (search online for suitable sites). How different is this from reading the text for yourself?

Despite these developments, the main mode of communication was still public performance. It is helpful to think of Chaucer's original audience as listening to *The Canterbury Tales* rather than reading them. No doubt Chaucer read his work to groups at court on frequent occasions, and his audience would have been a mix of different social groups and classes. In this sense Chaucer's situation would have been similar to that of Shakespeare, who had to construct dramas that would appeal to the widest possible taste and intellect. *The Canterbury Tales* includes plenty of entertaining moments to elicit the most superficial of responses, yet also contains subtle and sophisticated elements. Another development was that Chaucer was identified by name as an author and was popular in his own lifetime. Before this, almost all art was anonymous – it was the work of art that mattered, not its creator.

Purpose

This consideration of Chaucer's audience leads to the vexed question of Chaucer's intentions in composing *The Canterbury Tales*, a subject to which there is no definitive answer.

Irony

Irony is the dominant tone throughout *The Canterbury Tales*, and this makes Chaucer's work elusive and his purpose difficult to define. Irony always depends on personal interpretation, but not all interpretations are equally justifiable or defensible, so be sure that yours are based on wide and careful reading.

An example will illustrate the need for thought. Consider lines 401–02 of *The Wife of Bath's Prologue*:

Top ten quotation

> Deceite, weping, spinning God hath yive
> To wommen kindely, whil that they may live.
>
> (lines 401–02)

This sounds proverbial, and seems to be the typical kind of misogynistic utterance that one would expect in a male-dominated age. But it is spoken here by the Wife, apparently approvingly. She is happy to be thought deceitful and able to use tears to get what she wants. She is also a weaver, so takes pride in her 'spinning'. She takes the degrading remark and turns it to her own advantage. Or does she? Her deceitfulness is hardly a desirable characteristic, and the reader may condemn her for revelling in it. In quoting a misogynistic attitude for her own purposes, she also appears to confirm its truth. This kind of complexity is characteristic of *The Wife of Bath's Prologue* and *Tale*, and a sophisticated response is required from the reader.

Possible interpretations

Modern readers must make up their own minds as to what they are going to gain from studying Chaucer, and this is often a reflection of what they bring to their studies. You will probably find evidence for all the interpretations suggested below, but it is up to you to decide what Chaucer has to offer, and how he is to be interpreted in the twenty-first century.

Entertainment

Chaucer's tales are entertaining, and some readers wish to look no further than that. John Carrington, in *Our Greatest Writers and Their Major Works* (2003), says simply: 'Chaucer has no over-arching moral or philosophical intention', and that he 'is driven by a curiosity and sympathy for life that excludes the judgemental'.

Social comment

Many readers find some degree of comment on the behaviour and manners of medieval society. This could be anything from wry observation to serious satire, for example a satire on the three estates class system or a developed thesis on the nature of marriage.

Moral teaching

In the *Retraction* included at the end of *The Canterbury Tales*, Chaucer quotes from St Paul's comment in the New Testament that all literature contains a moral lesson.

Devotional literature

As a development of the previous point, readers may consider the Christian framework of *The Canterbury Tales* and the idea that it preaches specifically Christian doctrines. The vast majority of medieval literature is religious in this sense, for example the mystery plays, such as the Coventry and York Cycles, are based on Bible stories. *The Canterbury Tales* finishes with *The Parson's Tale*, a sermon about the seven deadly sins, encouraging many to interpret them as having a Christian message about behaviour and morality.

Allegory

Medieval people were familiar with allegory, in which a surface narrative contains one or more further parallel layers of meaning. Such ideas were familiar from Christ's parables in the Bible, and the whole Bible was interpreted allegorically in the Middle Ages.

Literary context

The framework of *The Canterbury Tales*

The General Prologue introduces *The Canterbury Tales* and establishes the framework that will underpin the diverse collection of tales that follows. It is worth considering the *Tales* as a whole to see what Chaucer was trying to achieve. It is well known that Chaucer left the work unfinished when he died in 1400, and it has traditionally been assumed that we have only fragments of what he would have eventually written.

The tales and their tellers

Chaucer's original plan, as revealed in *The General Prologue*, allowed for 30 pilgrims telling four tales each, making 120 tales in all. Only 24 tales exist, however, four of which are unfinished, and although as the *Tales* stand nearly every pilgrim tells a tale, they tell only one each.

It is clear that Chaucer drastically modified his original plan, although he never altered *The General Prologue* to confirm this. There is an excellent reason for his changes. In Chaucer's hands, the tales and tellers are matched with great care, so that one illuminates the other. This is conspicuously true of characters such as the Wife of Bath and the Pardoner. To give these characters more than one tale would gain nothing, and would in fact weaken the effectiveness of the link between tale and teller. In this way Chaucer breaks out of the traditional mould of story collections, in which the character of the narrator is largely unimportant; *The Thousand and One Nights*, for example, has a single narrator for all of its diverse stories.

The significance of the connection between the pilgrims and their tales is emphasised by the only character to tell two tales: Chaucer himself. He starts

> **TASK**
>
> As you read and review this Contexts chapter, make notes on the particular contexts that you feel cast light on *The Wife of Bath's Prologue* and *Tale*. Where possible, make specific reference to the text.

> **CRITICAL VIEW**
>
> It is possible to see Chaucer as an allegorist in whole or in part; Robert P. Miller, writing in the *Companion to Chaucer Studies* (1968), comments: 'Each pilgrim tells his tale from his own point of view, but this point of view is finally to be measured in the perspective afforded by the allegorical system' (p.277).

Build critical skills

Why might *The Canterbury Tales* be unfinished? Do you think the task of creating 30 individual narrators, with matching tales, was simply too ambitious, or was there another reason?

off with the tale of *Sir Thopas*, but this is told so feebly that the Host (hardly the most astute of critics) interrupts him and tells him to stop. Chaucer thereby achieves the double effect of satirising the weak and formulaic narrative verse of his own time and also creating a joke against himself. His revenge is to let the pilgrim Chaucer follow up with 'a lytel thing in prose', the extended and deeply moral *Tale of Melibee*. Given that the only other prose piece in *The Canterbury Tales* is *The Parson's Tale*, a meditation on penance, the author may well intend that the pilgrim Chaucer's tale be regarded as one of the most important pieces in the collection, although it is not at all to modern taste.

It is therefore likely that *The Canterbury Tales* is much nearer to completion than a consideration of Chaucer's original plan suggests. There are, however, certain anomalies that Chaucer would have needed to address:

- The Yeoman, the Ploughman and the Five Guildsmen lack tales. The absence of *The Ploughman's Tale* is a particular loss, given the iconic status of ploughmen, as established by Chaucer's contemporary William Langland in *Piers Plowman*.

- *The Cook's Tale* and *The Squire's Tale* are unfinished and simply break off partway through; the Knight interrupts the Monk, and the Host halts the doggerel tale of *Sir Thopas*.

- There are occasional discrepancies in the assignation of tales to tellers, for example *The Shipman's Tale* is clearly intended to have a female narrator.

- In several cases there is no significant connection between tale and teller, although this may be intentional.

- Some of the tales do not have links between them, and the final sequence of the tales is not established.

Taken as a whole, however, it is possible to discern a powerful and unified work that closely reflects Chaucer's final intentions.

Narrative device of the pilgrimage

The Canterbury Tales is based on two great defining structures: the story collection and the pilgrimage. The latter serves two purposes in the work. First, it is a narrative device, and second, it has a thematic function.

The role of pilgrimage in framing the narrative is simple but important. It gives Chaucer a basic plot – 30 pilgrims travel from London to Canterbury and back again – within which he can set out the multiple and varied narratives of his characters. It allows him to gather together a complete cross-section of the social hierarchy (excluding royalty, who would have travelled separately, and the lowest serfs, who would not have been able to leave their work), in circumstances in which the characters can mingle on terms of near equality. This equality would have existed with regard to their journey and experiences, but crucially there is also equality of opportunity; every pilgrim gets the chance to tell a story, and every story receives the same attention, although what the pilgrims choose to do with their opportunities is another matter. The pilgrimage is also dynamic, so that circumstances on the journey can impinge on the storytelling framework, as happens when the pilgrims encounter a canon whose yeoman tells a tale of his own.

Thematic function of the pilgrimage

The second function of the pilgrimage in *The Canterbury Tales* is even more important. A pilgrimage has two aspects: it is a journey, but it is also a sacred journey. Both elements are crucial to understanding of Chaucer's work.

Journeys

The image of the journey has always been central to human understanding. Life itself is conventionally seen as a journey from birth to death, and so any physical journey can be viewed as an image of life, with the travellers gaining experience as they progress. A pilgrimage is a special kind of physical journey, where the goal is a holy or sacred place. The parallel with the journey of life gains an extra significance, because the pilgrimage's sacred purpose is the equivalent of the soul's journey through life towards God. The best-known form of pilgrimage in modern times is the Muslim pilgrimage to Mecca, a journey that every devout Muslim is supposed to undertake at least once.

Holy sites and shrines

In the Middle Ages the pilgrimage was a common and popular activity and there were innumerable holy places to visit. The most holy site of all was Jerusalem, which the Wife of Bath visited three times, and Chaucer also mentions some of the other more famous ones, particularly Santiago de Compostela in Spain. In England, the shrine of Thomas Becket in Canterbury was the most popular destination following Becket's assassination in 1170, and it would remain so until it was destroyed by Henry VIII in the 1530s.

The importance of shrines lay in people's belief in the efficacy of saints and holy relics, as is evident from Chaucer's portrayal of the Pardoner. The Catholic Church taught that God could not be approached directly; it was therefore necessary to pray to those closest to him to intercede. Along with the Virgin Mary, with her unique position as the mother of Christ, the saints were thought to be endowed with special powers and influence. The relics of saints, particularly their bones, were held to have mystical, almost magical, powers, and there were dozens of shrines associated with particular saints, each usually venerated for a specific quality.

Travel

Pilgrimage therefore held an important place in medieval life, but it was also a way to travel. In an insecure world there was safety in numbers, as well as the pleasure of company. Some of Chaucer's pilgrims, such as the Guildsmen, would be delighted to have a Knight as part of the group, because he could offer practical as well as symbolic protection. A woman like the Wife of Bath would

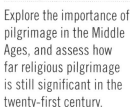

Taking it further ▶

Explore the importance of pilgrimage in the Middle Ages, and assess how far religious pilgrimage is still significant in the twenty-first century.

Taking it further ▶

Explore the importance of Thomas Becket further by doing an internet search. You could also investigate whether there was a medieval shrine or well-known saint near where you live.

be pleased that the Guildsmen themselves were there, among whom she might look for her sixth husband; it would also have been difficult for her as a woman to travel alone.

It has been said that medieval pilgrimages were the equivalent of modern-day package holidays, and there is some value in the analogy, at least if it is seen as indicating the impulse to travel and the willingness of diverse people to band together for convenience and economies of scale. The comparison falls down, however, when the purpose of travel is considered. Modern holidaymakers largely seek pleasure and few travel with an overtly spiritual purpose. The reverse was true in the Middle Ages; although a few of Chaucer's pilgrims might have had purely social or secular motives, most would have had a greater or lesser degree of devotion, and all would have been aware of the sacred significance of their journey, even if they sometimes chose to ignore it.

Symbolism

Build critical skills

Is a physical map of the pilgrimage important, or is the journey just a metaphorical one?

Every character, every tale, and every word of *The Canterbury Tales* is contained within the symbolic framework of the pilgrimage, whether the individual characters are aware of it or not. When the Parson tells his tale of sin and repentance the connection is obvious, but the symbolism of the pilgrimage is equally relevant when the Merchant is telling his tale of an ill-judged marriage, when the Miller and the Reeve are trading tales at each other's expense, or when the Pardoner tries to con his audience through the techniques that he has just exposed. Every one of these is measured against, and judged by, the sacred context in which their journey and their lives take place.

The route to Canterbury

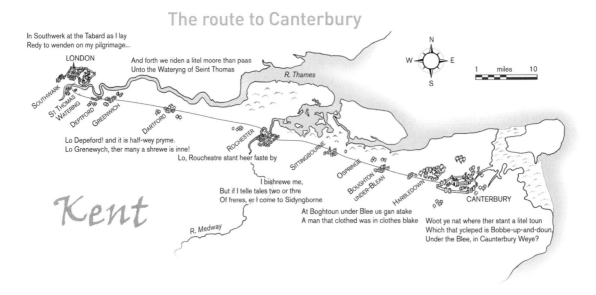

▲ The map shows the details of the pilgrimage in *The Canterbury Tales*, including the places mentioned by Chaucer in the text; the journey from London to Canterbury was nearly 60 miles and would usually have taken several days in each direction

The multiple narrators of *The Canterbury Tales*

In a conventional novel, the action is mediated to the reader by a narrator:

Narrator

Audience

In *The Canterbury Tales*, Chaucer introduces further narrative levels that offer the opportunity for much greater subtlety. First, Chaucer the author introduces himself as a character or persona within the text, so that the situation is as follows:

Chaucer the author

Chaucer the pilgrim

Audience

This means that when you come across a remark in *The General Prologue* such as 'And I seyde his opinion was good', it is ostensibly made by Chaucer the pilgrim. The reader must decide how far it may also be Chaucer the author's view.

When it comes to the tales themselves, a further layer of complexity is added because each tale is told by one of the pilgrims and is reported by Chaucer the pilgrim. The narrative therefore reaches its audience at three removes from its author:

Chaucer the author

Chaucer the pilgrim

Pilgrim narrator

Audience

Finally, when a character within one of the tales speaks, a fifth narrative layer is added:

Chaucer the author

Chaucer the pilgrim

Pilgrim narrator

Character

Audience

The attentive reader must decide how far each of the narrating figures is in accord with what is being said. For example, the old woman in *The Wife of Bath's Tale* comments during her lecture on 'gentillesse':

> Looke who that is moost vertuous always…
> Taak him for the grettest gentil man.

(lines 1113, 1116)

The reader needs to consider how far the old woman is being sincere (she is), how far the Wife of Bath endorses this view (she purports to, but it hardly reflects well on her own personality and behaviour), what Chaucer the pilgrim's view would be (probable agreement), and finally what Chaucer the author intends to convey about the nature of behaviour in the context of the whole of *The Wife of Bath's Prologue* and *Tale*. This last question is simultaneously the most important and, because of all the intervening narrative layers, the most difficult to decide, and it is why critical debate about Chaucer is unending.

Chaucer the pilgrim as narrator

The subtlety in Chaucer's craft arises from the device of the pilgrim narrator. This persona is portrayed as a sociable but rather diffident character. When the time comes for him to tell his own tale the Host thinks he looks 'elvyssh' (otherworldly) and shy: 'For evere upon the ground I se thee stare' (*Prologue to Sir Thopas*, line 697). Chaucer the pilgrim begins to tell a poor story (*Sir Thopas*), but once interrupted by the Host he launches into a long, moral, prose narrative (*Tale of Melibee*), which shows his erudition and seriousness. In *The General Prologue*, Chaucer the pilgrim frequently appears to be naive, most famously when he agrees with the Monk's low opinion of his own vows ('And I seyde his opinion was good', line 183). Often this encourages the other pilgrims to make further indiscreet confessions about their behaviour, such as the Monk revealing his obsession with hunting and riding. When Chaucer the pilgrim does wish to comment directly on a character, he can do so, as in the case of the Summoner: 'But wel I woot he lied right in dede' (line 661).

The 'marriage group' of tales

The term 'marriage group' was coined by the critic G.L. Kittredge in his seminal essay 'Chaucer's discussion of marriage', published in *Modern Philology Volume IX* (1911–12). Although some of his ideas now seem outdated, this remains an important discussion of Chaucer's work and intentions. You can find this essay on the internet at: http://sites.fas.harvard.edu/~chaucer (click on Site Index to find this essay). Kittredge claimed that there is a sequence of stories in *The Canterbury Tales* that forms a closely knit exploration of marriage. The sequence starts with *The Wife of Bath's Prologue* and *Tale* and, after a digression involving the Friar and the Summoner, is continued in the tales of the Clerk, Merchant, Squire and Franklin. The brief summary of these tales that follows helps to place *The Wife of Bath's Prologue* and *Tale* in its proper context.

The Wife of Bath's Prologue and Tale

The Wife's prologue, which at 800 lines is longer than many of the other pilgrims' tales, tells of her personal experience of marriage. She has had five husbands, and has treated them mercilessly, until the fifth fights back and reads anti-feminist writings to her, although he is eventually forced to concede 'maistrie' (mastery) to her. This prologue is an important setting for the ensuing debate about 'good' and 'bad' marriages.

The Wife of Bath then tells the tale of a knight who rapes a maiden. Condemned to death, he is given a year to find the answer to the question: 'What do women most desire?' He meets a hideous old hag who promises to give him the answer if he will do anything she asks. He is forced to agree and, having saved his life with the answer (that women most desire dominance over their husbands), she demands that he marry her. On their wedding night he is revolted by her appearance, but she reproaches him for his lack of knightly courtesy. She poses him a further challenge by offering to be ugly but faithful, or beautiful but potentially adulterous. Unable to choose, he grants her 'maistrie' over him, and is rewarded with her magical transformation into a beautiful and faithful young woman.

Taking it further ▶

Read Kittredge's essay and discuss it in class. How valid are the ideas expressed in it? How far does it reflect the values of the time at which it was written, shortly before the First World War?

The Friar's Tale

The Friar and the Summoner, who tell their tales next, do not tell tales that are part of the 'marriage group', but they are included here to show the sequencing of this part of *The Canterbury Tales*. Like the Miller and the Reeve, they are mutually antagonistic, and tell tales at each other's expense.

The Friar's tale is about a summoner who meets a devil in the guise of a yeoman. They agree to work as partners. When they come across a carter who is cursing his horses and wishes the devil would take them, the summoner invites the devil to take the carter at his word; the devil, however, is unable to snatch the horses because what the carter says is not what he truly wants. The summoner goes into a widow's house to demand money, and when she refuses he threatens to take her new pan instead. She wishes him and the pan to the devil; the devil asks her to confirm her wish, and when she does so he carries the summoner off to hell.

The Summoner's Tale

The Summoner, infuriated by the Friar, tells the story of a greedy friar who visits a bedridden man. The man protests that all his gifts to the friars have not aided his recovery, but the friar still asks him for a further donation. The man invites him to put his hand in his bed to receive a rich gift, but when the friar does so the 'gift' is a huge fart. The friar protests about this treatment to the lord of the village but gains little sympathy, and a young squire solves the problem of how the gift can be divided equally among the friars.

The Clerk's Tale

An Italian marquis, Walter, marries a beautiful young woman, Griselda, who promises that she will never willingly disobey him. After the birth of their daughter, Walter is seized with an urge to test Griselda's faithfulness; he has the baby taken away, and says it is going to be murdered. On the birth of a son, he does the same thing. Griselda patiently accepts all this, but Walter is not satisfied. He pretends to have their marriage annulled, says he wants a younger wife, and insists that Griselda attends the wedding. Griselda remains patient, and is rewarded with the return of her two children and the eternal faithfulness of Walter.

The Merchant's Tale

January, a 60-year-old knight and womaniser from Lombardy in Italy, decides to marry. He sends for his friends to advise him, and although he sounds pious he wants to marry quickly and to have a young wife. Ignoring what is said to him, he pursues his own desires, and finds a pretty young woman called May. They marry, and he hurries everyone away from the marriage feast so that he can enjoy his wedding night.

Meanwhile his young squire, Damyan, is himself sick with love for May. When January sends May to comfort him, the two exchange letters and seek an opportunity to meet. Their chance arrives when January suddenly becomes blind. Despite his jealousy and watchfulness, the lovers contrive a plot to meet in the garden where January spends time with May.

May prompts January to take her to the garden one day. She climbs a tree, where Damyan is already hidden, and they have sex. January's sight is magically restored, but May persuades him that this is a direct result of her actions and that he has a mistaken view of what has taken place. January accepts this and is overjoyed with his restored sight and with her.

The Squire's Tale

This is one of the unfinished stories in *The Canterbury Tales*, and is a **romance**. King Cambyuskan has a beautiful daughter, Candace. At a feast a strange knight appears, bearing magical gifts: a flying horse, a ring that enables the wearer to understand birds' speech, and a magical sword. Candace wears the ring and hears a falcon complaining because she has been deserted by her lover. Candace takes the falcon back to the palace. After an indication of some of what is to follow, the tale then breaks off.

Romance: a story of love and heroism, deriving from medieval court life and fairy tale.

The Franklin's Tale

For the critic Kittredge, this final tale in the group seems to offer the perfect solution to the marriage problem. A knight in Brittany, Arveragus, marries a lady, Dorigen, and they make an agreement that although Arveragus will maintain the illusion of male authority, in reality they will be equal partners. While he is away in England, Dorigen fears for his safe return because of the rocks on the coast. A young squire, Aurelius, promises to remove the rocks if she will love him, and in an unguarded moment she promises to do so. Aurelius pays a magician to make the rocks seemingly disappear, and claims Dorigen's love. Arveragus returns and says that she must keep her promise, but Aurelius, seeing her distress, frees her from her word. The magician in turn relinquishes his payment, and the Franklin celebrates the generosity of all the parties involved.

Analogues of *The Wife of Bath's Tale*

One of the most useful insights you can gain into medieval literature is an understanding of the way that stories were told and re-told until they were familiar to audiences. There are many references throughout this guide to the main analogues – that is, comparable versions – of *The Wife of Bath's Tale*, so the main ones are summarised here for convenience.

The Tale of Florent

A version with glossary and notes can be found at: http://d.lib.rochester.edu/teams/text/peck-gower-confessio-amantis-book-1#florent

Taking it further ▶

It is worth exploring the analogues. This may vary from looking briefly at them to see how they differ in form, structure, language and content from Chaucer's work, to an in-depth analysis of the relationship between them and *The Wife of Bath's Tale*. Although this is essentially undergraduate-style work, it might present opportunities for coursework.

A knight named Florent kills a man in self-defence. As a punishment the dead man's relatives set Florent the task of discovering 'what alle wommen most desire', or else he will be killed. He meets 'a lothly wommannysch figure' who offers the information, but only if he will promise to marry her. Florent is reluctant, but reflects that she is old and will probably die soon, so he agrees. She permits him to try other answers, but of course her answer is the correct one, that women want to rule over men ('be soverein of mannes love'), and Florent reluctantly has to keep to their agreement. He hides her from public view, however, and marries her in secret. On their wedding night he at first lies with his back to her, but when he turns over he discovers that she is beautiful. She offers him the choice, to have her beautiful either at night or during the day. Unable to decide, he leaves the choice to her. As a result the spell on her, cast by a wicked stepmother, is broken and she becomes beautiful all the time.

The Wedding of Sir Gawain and Dame Ragnelle

A version with glossary and notes can be found at: http://d.lib.rochester.edu/teams/text/hahn-sir-gawain-wedding-of-sir-gawain-and-dame-ragnelle

This is an Arthurian story. A mysterious knight, Sir Gromer Somer Joure, meets King Arthur hunting in a forest, and challenges him to discover what it is that women most desire ('Whate wemen desyren moste'). He gives him a year to find the answer, and threatens to kill him if he fails. Sir Gawain, King Arthur's nephew, suggests they travel to seek the solution, and each of them gathers possible answers in a book. Riding out one last time, Arthur encounters the hideously ugly Dame Ragnelle, who has a snotty nose, yellow teeth and bleary eyes. She offers him the true answer, if he will get Gawain to marry her. Gawain willingly agrees out of love for his king, and Dame Ragnelle tells Arthur that women most desire 'sovereynte'. Arthur returns to Sir Gromer and tries all the answers he and Gawain have collected, but in the end only Dame Ragnelle's answer is the true one. She and Gawain are married with great ceremony. On their wedding night she is transformed into a beautiful lady, but explains that she is under a spell and can be beautiful only either at night or during the day. Gawain grants her 'sovereynte' to choose which she prefers. This breaks the spell completely, and she becomes permanently beautiful and they are happily married.

The Marriage of Sir Gawain

A version of this ballad (Child Ballads number 31) with glossary and notes can be found at: http://d.lib.rochester.edu/teams/text/hahn-sir-gawain-marriage-of-sir-gawain

This ballad is similar in outline to *The Wedding of Sir Gawain and Dame Ragnelle*. It too features King Arthur, and a baron who demands he finds the answer to the riddle of 'what thing it is that a woman most desires'. Again Arthur and Gawain collect answers, but the true solution is given by a hideous hag. In this ballad Arthur offers that Gawain will marry her. Arthur returns to the baron, who rejects all answers apart from the hag's, that 'a woman will have her will'. As in the other versions, on their wedding night the hag becomes beautiful and offers Gawain the choice of having her fair by night or by day. He lets her 'have her will' in this, and again the spell is broken and she becomes his beautiful wife.

Critical context

All literary texts are subject to revaluation with the passage of time, and critical approaches will vary according to the concerns and preoccupations of the critic's period. Each student, quite properly, evaluates the text for themselves. Your own considered opinion is what matters, but it should be based on the most detailed and measured analysis of which you are capable. *The Wife of Bath's Prologue* and *Tale* is a fertile ground for varied critical approaches because there is so much controversy about the text and the nature of the Wife of Bath herself. As a result, it is possible to identify a range of critical stances that have been taken over time.

Historical criticism and New Historicism

Historical critics tend to look at *The Canterbury Tales* as entirely a product of its time, and look at it solely within its original context. Some early critics even tried to find real-life counterparts of Chaucer's pilgrims, whereas others looked at Chaucer in terms of medieval literary schemes such as allegory, or the representation of what was called Estates Satire, examining the nature of society at the time. New Historicists look further afield, to the whole cultural background of texts, attempting to see how texts were formed by and how they reflected the historical, political, economic and social circumstances within which they were written. Putting the Wife of Bath in her contemporary context offers a fascinating insight into the changing place and status of women in the later Middle Ages.

Marxist criticism

Marxist critics look for what literary texts have to say about the power relations between various classes or economic groups within society. Chaucer's work is a rich source of material because it appears to be written at a time when many of the traditional models of interrelationship, particularly the concepts embodied in feudalism, were breaking down, and society was metamorphosing into something more recognisably modern. The Wife of Bath can easily be seen to symbolise this transition. She is not easily classified, having independent means and using her gender to forge a role in society that contrasts with expected norms. She challenges the accepted hierarchies and power structures of her time. She seems to view everything, including marriage, sex and even love, in material terms, as business transactions.

Context

King Henry (Child Ballads 32) is yet another version, featuring King Henry as the noble knight who has to fulfil the wishes of a hideous hag. A memorable version by the folk/rock group Steeleye Span can be seen on YouTube, and their version of the lyrics can be found by an internet search.

CRITICAL VIEW

The most complete, easily available resource that examines critical approaches directly in relation to *The Wife of Bath's Prologue* and *Tale* is Peter G. Beidler's *The Wife of Bath*, in the series *Case Studies in Contemporary Criticism* (Bedford/St Martin's, 1996). This contains extensive coverage of each approach, with introductions, essays and bibliographies.

Psychoanalytic criticism

The apparent roundness of the Wife of Bath's character makes her an obvious candidate for psychoanalytic criticism, which attempts to subject literary characters to the same kind of forensic analysis as would be applied to real human beings. It is easy to dismiss this approach, since a literary construct manifestly is exactly that – an artificial construct produced by an author for a particular purpose. In the Middle Ages this was certainly true; characters were often severely limited in scope, perhaps metaphorically or allegorically representing a single characteristic or idea. A psychoanalytic approach can, however, promote valuable insights if caution is exercised about the method. The Wife of Bath can be seen to represent a liberated spirit throwing off the shackles of male repression, or to represent a nymphomaniac who needs constant sexual gratification and will manipulate men to ensure she gains it. This is a modern way of looking at a medieval work, and discretion should be exercised in evaluating its worth.

Deconstructionist criticism

This is perhaps the most difficult type of literary theory for students to grasp because it challenges the idea that texts can offer 'true' meanings. It is based on the idea that the nature of language itself means that words cannot be tied to precise significations. For this reason every reading of a text can be challenged by a counter-reading, and meaning remains elusive or indefinable. In the case of *The Wife of Bath's Prologue* and *Tale* this can lead to the stripping away of notions of character and characterisation to examine the uncertainties and ambiguities contained in the language Chaucer uses.

Feminist criticism

It is inevitable that feminist critics should be drawn to the Wife of Bath. She so evidently proclaims the power and freedom of her sex, and openly defies the conventional wisdom and expectations of her age. She is perhaps the proto-feminist *par excellence* in earlier English literature. She gives a voice to all the women of the Middle Ages, who otherwise are almost completely unheard.

The situation, of course, is not that simple. The Wife is the creation of a male writer. Her discourse is built from a tapestry of anti-feminist writings, and she can sometimes be seen as the epitome of all the things those writers are complaining about.

Feminist criticism inevitably operates from a historical perspective, from a time when feminist ideology and feminist concerns have risen in society's consciousness. Chaucer's own audience could not have foreseen how the role of women would develop and change over the ensuing centuries.

Taking it further ▷

All the critical approaches should be considered as you develop your own response to *The Wife of Bath's Prologue* and *Tale*, but you may want to explore further those approaches that seem to you to be most valid. Continually bear in mind that you will be extending your ability to fulfil the demands of AOs 3 and 5.

Working with the text

Assessment Objectives and skills

The five key English Literature Assessment Objectives (AOs) describe the different skills you need to show in order to get a good grade. Regardless of what texts or which examination specification you are following, the AOs lie at the heart of your study of English literature at AS and A-level; they let you know exactly what the examiners are looking for and provide a helpful framework for your literary studies.

The Assessment Objectives require you to:

AO1	Articulate informed, personal and creative responses to literary texts, using associated concepts and terminology, and coherent, accurate written expression.
AO2	Analyse ways in which meanings are shaped in literary texts.
AO3	Demonstrate understanding of the significance and influence of the contexts in which literary texts are written and received.
AO4	Explore connections across literary texts.
AO5	Explore literary texts informed by different interpretations.

The weighting for each AO varies between boards and between tasks; for example, comparative non-examination assessment tasks (coursework) will always place greater weight on AO4. Overall, however, AOs 1–3 bear the greatest proportion of marks and this should be kept under consideration. Try to bear in mind that the AOs are there to support rather than to restrict you; do not look at them as encouraging a tick-box approach or a mechanistic reductive way into the study of literature. Examination questions are written with the AOs in mind, so if you answer them clearly and carefully you should automatically hit the right targets. If you are devising your own questions for NEA, seek the help of your teacher to ensure that your essay title is carefully worded to liberate the required Assessment Objectives so that you can do your best.

Although the Assessment Objectives are common to all the exam boards, each specification differs in the way it meets the requirements. The boards' websites provide useful information, including sections for students, past papers, sample papers and mark schemes. You are advised to make use of them.

- AQA: www.aqa.org.uk
- Edexcel: www.edexcel.com
- OCR: www.ocr.org.uk
- WJEC: www.wjec.co.uk

Remember, though, that your knowledge and understanding of the text still lies at the heart of A-level study, as it always has done. In the end, the study of literature starts with, and comes back to, your own engagement with the text itself. It is your informed personal response that will be judged and rewarded.

AO1	Articulate informed, personal and creative responses to literary texts, using associated concepts and terminology, and coherent, accurate written expression.

AO1 focuses upon literary and critical insight, organisation of material and clarity of written communication. Examiners are looking for accurate spelling and grammar and clarity of thought and expression, so say what you want to say and say it as clearly as you can.

Aim for cohesion; your ideas should be presented coherently with an overall sense of a developing argument. Think carefully about your introduction, because your opening paragraph not only sets the agenda for your response but provides the reader with a strong first impression of you – whether positive or negative. Note the requirement to provide a 'personal' response. Your essay should not sound as if you are repeating other people's ideas; it should demonstrably be the work of somebody who has studied the text carefully, read and listened to others' opinions (including teachers and critical sources – see AO5), and who has then formed their own views and responses.

You can write in either the first person or the third person, as you prefer, but the sense of your own critical voice should emerge clearly. Try to use appropriate 'associated terminology' but do not hide behind fancy critical terms or complicated language that you do not fully understand; 'feature-spotting' and merely listing literary terms is a classic mistake that all examiners are familiar with. Choose your references carefully; writing out great gobbets of a text you have learned by heart underlines your inability to select the choicest short quotation with which to clinch your argument. Instead, incorporate brief quotations into your own sentences, weaving them in seamlessly to illustrate your points and develop your argument.

The hallmarks of a well written essay – whether for NEA or in an exam – include a clear and coherent introduction that orientates the reader, a systematic and logical argument, aptly chosen and neatly embedded quotations, and a conclusion that consolidates your case.

All types of essay require high order skills for AO1 and you must pay great attention to your essay-writing ability.

> **A02** Analyse ways in which meanings are shaped in literary texts.

The key to gaining marks for A02 is to be able to demonstrate how form, structure (how the text is organised, how its constituent parts connect with each other) and language 'shape meanings'. If 'form is meaning', what are the implications of Chaucer's decision to select this specific genre, and what are the implications of the fact that the Wife of Bath's contribution is just a small part of *The Canterbury Tales*? In terms of structure, in the case of *The Wife of Bath's Prologue* and *Tale*, why does Chaucer choose the bipartite structure of long prologue and shorter tale, and how do the two interact and support each other? In terms of language features, what is most striking about aspects such as dialogue, imagery and symbolism?

In order to discuss language in detail you will need to quote from the text – but the mere act of quoting is not enough to meet A02. What is important is what you do with the quotation – how you analyse it and how it illuminates your argument. Moreover, since you will often need to make points about larger generic and organisational features of the text, being able to reference effectively is just as important as mastering the art of the embedded quotation.

As with A01, fulfilling the A02 requirements is fundamental to gaining a high grade in all kinds of essays.

> **A03** Demonstrate understanding of the significance and influence of the contexts in which literary texts are written and received.

A03, with its emphasis on the 'significance and influence of the contexts in which literary texts are written and received', might at first seem less deeply rooted in the text itself. In fact, however, you are considering and evaluating here the relationship between the text and its contexts. Note the word 'received': this refers to the way interpretation can be influenced by the specific contexts within which the reader is operating; when you are studying a medieval text, there is a considerable gulf between its original contemporary context of production and the twenty-first century context in which you are receiving it.

To access A03 successfully you need to think about how contexts of production, reception, literature, culture, biography, geography, society, history, genre and **intertextuality** can affect texts. This can sound daunting when you are studying an author as distant in time as Chaucer, which is why this guide seeks to provide an insight into the contexts you need. Do not panic. Simply place the text at the heart of the web of contextual factors that you feel have had the

The influential French feminist and literary theorist Julia Kristeva (b. 1941) coined the term **'intertextuality'** in 1966 to describe the complex network of links which exist between texts.

most impact upon it; examiners want to see a sense of contextual alertness woven seamlessly into the fabric of your essay, rather than a clumsy bolted-on rehash of a website or your old history notes. By being aware of the age in which Chaucer was writing, you will naturally convey your understanding of the fact that literary works contain embedded and encoded representations of the cultural, moral, religious, racial and political values of the society from which they emerged, and that over time attitudes and ideas can change until the views they reflect are no longer widely shared. There is also significant overlap between a focus on interpretations (AO5) and a focus on contexts, so do not think about trying to pigeonhole the AOs.

One of the advantages of studying Chaucer is that you cannot avoid talking about its contexts, both the ones in which it was originally received and how modern readers respond to it. It is always fruitful to compare medieval and modern attitudes and approaches, and is sensible to recognise the different responses that might occur in any era. *The Wife of Bath's Prologue* and *Tale* is popular because it seems to present us with a 'proto-feminist' – a woman arguing for women's rights six centuries ahead of her time. Such a view is seductive but highly misleading, and you need to develop a much more sophisticated response. The Wife of Bath is not a feminist, because she argues for much more than female equality. She demands absolute control over her men and in this sense is no better than any man demanding complete control over women.

Contexts are important since much will depend on the depth of your understanding of medieval art and its purpose, together with the modern standpoint from which you yourself approach the issues. Learn about the former by studying the 'Contexts' section of this guide, and be honest and self-aware in examining the latter.

CRITICAL VIEW

The critic James Winny, in his 1994 edition of the text, sees the Wife of Bath as someone who has 'contested the prohibitive morality of the medieval Church and planted her own pragmatic doctrine on the ruins' (p.15). You might regard Winny's comment as completely misunderstanding how medieval literature works. He has, in any case, altered his own opinion. The quotation is from his 1994 revised edition, but Winny's original 1965 edition claimed that she had '*overthrown* the prohibitive morality of the medieval Church' (p.15, italics added) rather than merely 'contested' it. You should be encouraged that critics also modify their views in the light of longer study, so never be afraid to re-examine your own readings and interpretations.

A04   Explore connections across literary texts.

Clearly, the way you meet AO4 will depend on whether you are studying *The Wife of Bath's Prologue* and *Tale* as an exam text or for coursework. You will find it easier to make comparisons and connections between texts (of any kind) if you try to balance them as you write; remember also that connections and comparisons are not just about finding similarities – differences are just as interesting. Above all, consider how the comparison illuminates each text. It is not only a matter of finding the relationships and connections, but of analysing what they show. When writing comparatively use words and constructions that will help you link your texts, such as *whereas, on the other hand, while, in contrast, by comparison, as in, differently, similarly, comparably.*

While you do have to write about a named passage and another one of your own choosing, AO4 is not tested by questions on *The Wife of Bath's Prologue* and *Tale* set by Edexcel.

Inevitably, AO4 is of major importance if you are undertaking a non-examination assessment task. Your choice of text for comparison should specifically allow you to meet AO4 fully. In order for that to happen, there must be strong and clear areas of comparison, in terms of theme (for example relationships or gender dominance) and/or character. Bear in mind that in this regard strongly contrasted texts may work as well as, or better than, similar ones. A modern novel with a strongly dominant male protagonist may offer many starting points for comparison with Chaucer, with the additional benefit that the genre (novel v. poetry) may also be a factor in the effect of the texts.

A05   Explore literary texts informed by different interpretations.

To access AO5 effectively you need to measure your own interpretation of a text against those of your teacher and other readers, particularly critical sources. By all means refer to named critics and quote from them if it seems appropriate, but the examiners are most interested in your informed *personal* response. If your teacher takes a particular critical line, be prepared to challenge and question it; there is nothing more dispiriting for an examiner than to read a set of scripts from one centre that all say exactly the same thing. Top candidates produce fresh, personal responses (see AO1) rather than merely regurgitating the ideas of others, however famous or insightful their interpretations may be.

Of course, your interpretation will be convincing only if it is supported by clear reference to the text, and you will be able to evaluate other readers' ideas only if you test them against the evidence of the text itself. A worthwhile AO5 answer means more than quoting someone else's point of view and saying you agree, although it can be helpful to use critical views if they push forward an argument of your own and you can offer relevant textual support. Look for other ways of reading texts – from a Marxist, feminist, new historicist, post-structuralist, psychoanalytic, dominant or oppositional point of view – that are more creative and original than merely copying out the ideas of just one person. Ideally, try to show an awareness of multiple readings with regard to your chosen text and an understanding that the meaning of a text is dependent as much upon what the reader brings to it as what the writer left there. Using modal verb phrases, such as *may be seen as*, *might be interpreted as* or *could be represented as*, implies that you are aware that different readers interpret texts in different ways at different times. The key word here is plurality: there is no single meaning, no right answer, and you need to evaluate a range of other ways of making textual meanings as you work towards your own.

AO5 is not tested directly by questions on *The Wife of Bath's Prologue* and *Tale* set by Edexcel. However, engaging with other opinions and critical viewpoints is likely to help you to articulate an informed personal response (AO1). In a non-examination assessment task, judicious reference to one or more critics can provide the spark to build a really persuasive case showing your personal response – particularly if you show yourself to be in disagreement! Do not, however, quote other people's opinions because you do not have any of your own.

Building skills 1: Structuring your writing

This section focuses on organising your written responses to convey your ideas as clearly and effectively as possible: the 'how' of your writing as opposed to the 'what'. More often than not, if your knowledge and understanding of *The Wife of Bath's Prologue* and *Tale* is sound, a disappointing mark or grade will be down to one of two common mistakes: misreading the question or failing to organise your response economically and effectively. In an examination you will normally use only a little of what you know about *The Wife of Bath's Prologue* and *Tale*; but if you focus your knowledge correctly, that's all you will need to gain full marks.

Understanding your assessment

It's important to prepare for the specific type of response your examination body sets with regard to *The Wife of Bath's Prologue* and *Tale*. You need to know whether you are studying the text as part of a non-examined assessment unit or as an examination set text. The format of your assessment has major implications for the way you organise your response and it dictates the depth and detail required to achieve a top band mark. In either case you need to quote relevantly, accurately and extensively. To gain a high mark, you are expected to focus in detail on specific passages, and your essay must be wholly and consistently relevant to the title selected. Make sure that the work is entirely your own; copying unacknowledged material from any source will lead to examiners referring your paper to the examining body for possible plagiarism.

Planning and beginning: locate the debate

A very common type of exam question invites you to open up a debate about the text by using various trigger words and phrases, such as 'Consider the view that …', 'Some readers think that …' or 'How far do you agree with the view that …?' When answering this type of question, the one thing you can be sure of is that exam questions never offer a view that makes no sense at all or one so blindingly obvious that all anyone can do is agree with it; there will always be a genuine interpretation at stake. Similarly, many non-examined assessment tasks are written to include a stated view to help give some shape to your writing. Logically, then, your introduction needs to orientate the reader by addressing the terms of this debate and sketching out the outlines of how you intend to move the argument forward. Since it's obviously going to be helpful if you actually know this before you start writing, you really do need to plan before you begin to write.

Undertaking a lively debate about some of the ways in which *The Wife of Bath's Prologue* and *Tale* has been and can be interpreted is the DNA of your essay. Of course any good argument needs to be honest, but to begin by writing 'Yes, I totally agree with this obviously true statement' suggests a fundamental misunderstanding of what studying literature is all about. Any stated view is designed to open up critical conversations, not to shut them down.

Plan your answer by collecting together points for and against the given view. Aim to see a stated opinion as an interesting way of focusing on a key facet of the text, as the following student has done.

Student A

As part of her non-examined assessment unit, this student is comparing *The Wife of Bath's Prologue* and *Tale* and *Mansfield Park* by Jane Austen, in order to explore this question:

How far do you agree that social environments are as important as personal characteristics in an author's creation of character?

At first glance one might argue that Fanny Price is moulded by her social environment, whereas it is the Wife of Bath who moulds hers. However, I would argue that this is superficial, and in fact in both cases the authors have used the social circumstances of the protagonist as a way of defining and structuring their character. Chaucer and Austen create characters who each have a strong set of personal values (albeit very different ones), and then place them in settings where these values can be examined and tested. Clearly, in the end, it is through the integration of personal characteristics and social situation that the characters are fully realised. The Wife of Bath is as much a 'victim' of her social position in the fourteenth century as Fanny is within the confines of early-nineteenth-century upper-class society. When the Wife walks 'from hous to hous, although he had it sworn', Chaucer uses the social conventions of the day to pinpoint the nature of her rebellious character. He shows her as being in constant tension with her social position; far from being a subservient wife, she is sexually dominant: 'How pitously a-night I made hem swinke!' Austen uses the identical technique when Henry Crawford unexpectedly visits Portsmouth, because Fanny's character is delineated by her sense of placement within the social context. She feels 'shame for the home in which he found her'; although this is her native environment, she has moved beyond it through her association with Mansfield Park, and is ashamed of her birth family.

Examiner's commentary

This student:

- ❧ expresses a confident and original personal view, arguing against a superficially attractive reading and showing her understanding of alternative interpretations; addresses AO1 and AO5

- ❧ shows a strong sense of the contexts of the texts, and can explore the connections between them, meeting AO3 and AO4

- ❧ knows that all quotations – whether from the texts or from secondary sources – are included within the word limit for the NEA unit, so integrates quotations within sentence structures

- ❧ demonstrates a clear awareness of the distinction between authors and characters, and the techniques used by authors to create character (one would expect the essay to develop to show how the authors use characters to explore themes).

If the rest of her essay reached this level of performance, it is likely she would be on course to achieve a notional grade A.

Student B

Student B is writing an answer to this Edexcel-style A-level examination question:

Explore attitudes to sexuality in *The Wife of Bath's Prologue* and *Tale*, by referring to lines 596–610 and one other passage of similar length.

You must discuss relevant contextual factors.

The student has chosen to compare lines 95–110.

The Wife of Bath boasts in line 608 that she 'hadde the beste quoniam mighte be', and this is the key to her character and to her sexuality. She is sexually promiscuous, and proud of it. At this point in her prologue she is unashamedly ogling Jankin even while following her late husband's coffin. It is fruitful to contrast this passage with lines 95–110, where she sets out the 'traditional' view of the virtues of virginity, as espoused by the Catholic Church at the time. She states in line 105 that 'virginitee is greet perfection', in accordance with Paul's teachings in the New Testament. In this earlier passage it seems as if she accepts conventional Catholic doctrine, but merely thinks that it is not appropriate for her. Chaucer's presentation of these two extreme attitudes to sexuality – virginity v. promiscuity – underlies the whole purpose of The Wife of Bath's Prologue and Tale. Chaucer tacitly demands that the reader makes a judgement, whether to side with the 'liberated' views of the Wife or with the 'traditional' views of the Church. This choice holds good for both medieval and modern readers, and is in line with the whole methodology of The Canterbury Tales; in The General Prologue, Chaucer has presented himself as a persona who judges his fellow pilgrims, and like him we may say the Wife's 'opinion was good', or that she 'lyed right in dede'.

Examiner's commentary

This student:

▼ has chosen an effective passage for comparison, a necessity when answering this type of question

▼ has set up the contrast between the two passages clearly with the neat formulation 'virginity v. promiscuity'

▼ has fluently integrated quotations into the syntax of the essay

▼ shows an impressive awareness of the wider context of Chaucer's technique in *The Canterbury Tales* as a whole

▼ has expressed himself well, although the wording could be more concise. This could become an issue in the confines of an examination essay.

If the rest of his essay reached this level of performance, it is likely he would be on course to achieve a notional grade A. Much depends on how the argument is developed.

Developing and linking: go with the flow

An essay is a very specific type of formal writing and requires an appropriate discourse structure. In the main body of your writing, you need to thread your developing argument through each paragraph consistently and logically, referring back to the terms established by the question itself, rephrasing and reframing as you go. It can be challenging to sustain the flow of your essay and keep firmly on track, but here are some techniques to help you:

- Ensure your essay doesn't disintegrate into a series of disconnected building blocks by creating a neat and stable bridge between one paragraph and the next.

- Use discourse markers – linking words and phrases, like *on the other hand*, *however*, *although* and *moreover* – to hold the individual paragraphs of your essay together and to signpost the connections between different sections of your overarching argument.

- Having set out an idea in Paragraph A, in Paragraph B you might then need to support it by providing a further example; if so, signal this to the reader with a phrase, such as: '**Moreover**, this imagery of the "fruit of marriage" can also be seen when …'

- To change direction and challenge an idea begun in Paragraph A by acknowledging that it is open to interpretation, you could begin Paragraph B with something like: '**On the other hand**, this view of the text could be challenged by a feminist critic …'

- Another typical paragraph-to-paragraph link is when you want to show that the original idea doesn't give the full picture. Here you could modify your original point with something like: '**Although** it is possible to see the Wife of Bath as an early feminist, this view needs to be set against the prevailing culture of the fourteenth century …'

Student C

As part of her non-examined assessment unit this student, like Student A, is comparing *The Wife of Bath's Prologue* and *Tale* with *Mansfield Park* by Jane Austen, in order to explore the question:

How far do you agree that social environments are as important as personal characteristics in an author's creation of character?

The Wife of Bath quotes a lot of anti-feminist texts that show the attitudes of society of her time, and she's aware that her behaviour isn't in accordance with religious guidance, but she doesn't care. When her husband quotes a proverb at her, she replies: 'I sette noght an hawe / of his proverbs n'of his olde sawe'. This shows that she rebels against the social conventions of her time. By contrast Fanny Price is always keen to uphold social convention, and afraid of breaching it. Her refusal to act in the play – 'No, indeed, Mr Bertram, you must excuse me' – is because she thinks Sir Thomas would disapprove, and it shows her moral stance as clearly as that of the Wife of Bath.

Examiner's commentary

This student:

◥ has the basis of a worthwhile point, but it has not been precisely focused and developed

◥ is able to select and use relevant quotations, although the ones chosen are neither as apt nor as well integrated into sentences as those of Student A

◥ achieves a clear comparison between the two texts, indicated by the use of 'by contrast'

◥ does not make clear that it is the author who creates the effects; she speaks only about the characters.

If the rest of her essay reached this level of performance, it is likely this student would be on course to achieve a notional grade C or D.

Student D

Like Student B, this student is writing an answer to the examination question:

Explore attitudes to sexuality in *The Wife of Bath's Prologue* and *Tale*, by referring to lines 596–610 and one other passage of similar length.

You must discuss relevant contextual factors.

She has chosen to compare lines 95–110.

Although some critics like D.W. Robertson have argued that the Wife of Bath is a medieval type, I think it is easy to see the hallmarks of true personality in her characterisation. She sounds like a preacher when she says 'Virginitee is greet perfection', but immediately contradicts this by saying in her own voice: 'He spak to them that wolde live parfitly; / And lordinges, by your leve, that am nat I.' She thereby asserts her own claim to sexual freedom against the teaching of the age, and is even more explicit in lines 609–10, where she calls on astrology rather than religion as her justification: 'I am al Venerien / In feeling, and myn herte is Marcien.' The sense of personality is confirmed by her language, which is at best informal ('al myn heret I yaf unto his hoold') and frequently colloquial: 'I had alwey a coltes *tooth' or 'As help me God! I was a lusty oon'. We believe that her open defence of sexual promiscuousness is sincere because it is couched in such vivid terms.*

Examiner's commentary

This student:

- has the material and her argument well under control, using quotation freely and effectively in support of points
- identifies an alternative reading in order to dismiss it and develop a strong, well-informed personal response
- shows contextual understanding in the comment about 'a medieval type' (but would need to explore contextual aspects in more depth elsewhere in the essay)
- moves freely between the two passages, showing her ability to connect and compare
- uses structural markers like 'although' and 'confirmed' in order to indicate the flow of the argument
- expresses herself clearly and precisely.

If the rest of her essay reached this level of performance, it is likely she would be on course to achieve a notional grade A.

Concluding: seal the deal

As you bring your writing to a close, you need to capture and clarify your response to the given view and make a relatively swift and elegant exit. Keep your final paragraph short and sweet. Now is not the time to introduce any new points – but equally, don't just reword everything you have already said either. Neat potential closers include:

- Looping the last paragraph back to something you mentioned in your introduction to suggest that you have now said all there is to say on the subject.
- Reflecting on your key points in order to reach a balanced overview.
- Ending with a punchy quotation that leaves the reader thinking.
- Discussing the contextual implications of the topic you have debated.
- Reversing expectations and ending on an interesting alternative view.
- Stating why you think the main issue, theme or character under discussion is so central to the text.
- Mentioning how different audiences over time might have responded to the topic you have been debating.

Student E

As part of his non-examined assessment unit this student, like Students A and C, is comparing *The Wife of Bath's Prologue* and *Tale* and *Mansfield Park* by Jane Austen, in order to explore the question:

How far do you agree that social environments are as important as personal characteristics in an author's creation of character?

It has been demonstrated that Fanny is not the 'simple, accepting figure' that the critic Andrew Wright claims she is, but rather is a complex character whose interactions with her environment are affected by her constantly evolving social status. I have shown how Austen charts these changes, and makes Fanny's eventual suitability as Edmund's wife plausible. Equally, I have sought to discredit Louise Fradenburg's application of psychoanalytical principles to the Wife of Bath, and conclude that she is not a Freudian 'subject' at all, but merely a mouthpiece for Chaucer's evaluation of the position of women in medieval society. She is a static character with unchanging views, not one who grows and develops like Fanny Price, and there lies the difference between fourteenth- and nineteenth-century literature.

Examiner's commentary

This student:

- ▼ concludes the essay strongly with a clear statement of his critical position in relation to the two texts and the comparison between them
- ▼ uses neatly expressed references to critics both to frame his own argument and to show his awareness of alternative interpretations
- ▼ uses a neat final encapsulation of his argument, which may be too sweeping but is effective in the context of the essay
- ▼ writes with flair and precision of vocabulary, and a strong personal voice.

If the rest of his essay reached this level of performance, it is likely this student would be on course to achieve a notional grade A.

Student F

Like Students B and D, this student is writing an answer to this examination question:

Explore attitudes to sexuality in *The Wife of Bath's Prologue* and *Tale*, by referring to lines 596–610 and one other passage of similar length.

You must discuss relevant contextual factors.

He has chosen to compare lines 882–98.

I think the Wife of Bath is trying to show how men are always in the wrong, and how she's always in the right. In the prologue she argues for sexual freedom and the dominance of women, and the tale acts as a kind of exemplar to show what happens when a man tries to get the upper hand. The knight's rape is symbolic of male dominance, and he must be taught a lesson. It's only when he gives in to the woman at the end that he is rewarded. This is an exact parallel to what happens at the end of the prologue, with the husband's submission to the Wife. Chaucer presents this twice in order to reinforce the argument. The two passages are a key to understanding this process and it can be argued that the Wife of Bath is a very modern woman under a medieval wimple. She could be said to be the first feminist.

Examiner's commentary

This student:

- ❐ has reached a clear conclusion about sexuality in the text, but this is couched in over-emphatic, black-and-white terms; a more nuanced approach would gain higher marks
- ❐ shows an awareness of Chaucer's craft, specifying that it is the author (rather than the character) who is achieving these effects
- ❐ shows little or no contextual understanding, and is in danger of regurgitating undigested pre-taught phrases ('a kind of exemplar', 'the first feminist') without locating them within the argument
- ❐ tries to find a striking final expression to round off the essay, but has not apparently justified it.

If the rest of his essay reached this level of performance, it is likely this student would be on course to achieve a notional grade C or D.

Building skills 2: Analysing texts in detail

Having worked through the 'Structuring your writing' section, you should now focus on this section of the guide to see how to obtain higher marks. It contains a range of annotated extracts from students' responses to *The Wife of Bath's Prologue* and *Tale* and extended commentaries. The next few pages will enable you to assess the extent to which these students have successfully demonstrated their writing skills and mastery of the Assessment Objectives, to provide you with an index by which to measure your own skills progress.

Each extract comes with a commentary to help you identify what the student is doing well and/or what changes they would need to make to their writing in order to target a higher grade.

The main focus here is on the ways in which you can successfully include within your own well-structured writing clear and appropriate references both to *The Wife of Bath's Prologue* and *Tale* itself and to the ways in which other readers have responded to the text. In an examination, of course, the 'other reading' you need to refer to consistently is that which is expressed in the question itself. In a non-examined assessment response, you will have more choice about which interpretations of the text you most want to work with – but since you have much more time and may well have written your own question title, you have no excuse to wander off task.

Analysis in examination tasks

Student G

This student is answering a sample examination task. The question, which is in the style of those set by Edexcel and specifically invites the student to 'explore' the text, is:

Explore the ways in which the concept of age is presented in *The Wife of Bath's Prologue* and *Tale*. Examine lines 455–75 and one other passage of similar length.

You must discuss relevant contextual factors.

The student in this case has chosen lines 1083–103 to compare.

Chaucer's vision of the young Alysoun, 'stibourn and strong, and joly as a pie', is deliberately created so that it can be contrasted with visions of age. In particular, the youthful image is set against the seminal moment in the tale when the knight has to confess why he refuses to embrace his wife. His devastating complaint – 'thou art so loothly, and so oold also' – makes her age as much as her repulsiveness the key issue. Chaucer's craft is conspicuously on display here. The moment resonates because of its brevity and directness, and because of the colloquial and abrupt language of the knight (so far removed from 'courtly' utterance). The long, drawn-out vowels of 'loothly' and 'oold' seem like a cry of anguish. The response of Chaucer's audience, whether medieval or modern, young or old, will be highly influenced by their circumstances. Young (A-level!) students might share the knight's horror of age; older readers (or listeners) might be dismissive.

This is why the process of ageing is so important, and so emphasised by Chaucer. He shows us the Wife as both a young woman 'ful of ragerie' and as a nostalgic old woman where age has 'biraft my beautee and my pith'. Her vision of her younger days is clearly rose-tinted, as she deploys bird similes to invoke her vision of a carefree independent existence like a '[mag]pie' and a 'nightingale'. Chaucer is intensely aware of these psychological aspects, because the tale is given as her wish fulfilment; the 'loothly' and 'so oold' lady is finally rejuvenated: 'she so fair was, and so yong therto'. It is a complex effect, and is likely to evoke complex responses in his audience, who will be either younger people fearing ageing, or older people being asked to look back. Nobody escapes the effects of time, which is why The Wife of Bath's Prologue and Tale speaks to us all.

Examiner's commentary

This student:

- refers back to the terms of the question frequently, keeping the question constantly in focus
- is clear that it is Chaucer who is the maker of textual meaning, specifically referring to his use of language as well as content
- is confident and persuasive in her comparison of the prologue and the tale
- forges a very clear link ('This is why …') between her two paragraphs, which achieves cohesion and reassures the examiner that she is still fully on task
- is in full command of her own written expression, using language succinctly and purposefully
- quotes frequently and always relevantly, and seamlessly embeds short snippets of quotation within her own sentences, so that the flow of her writing is not disrupted
- is fully aware of multiple audiences, medieval and modern, young and old (though detailed comment that uses contextual understanding would be required elsewhere in the response).

If the rest of her examination answer reached this level of performance, it is likely this student would be on course to achieve a notional grade A.

Student H

This student is answering a sample examination task. The question, which specifically invites the student to 'explore' the text, is:

Explore how male behaviour is presented in *The Wife of Bath's Prologue* and *Tale*. Examine lines 882–98 and one other passage of similar length.

The student in this case has chosen lines 983–99 to compare.

At the beginning of the tale the knight is sure of himself when he rapes the woman. He knows what he's doing and doesn't give a fig for the consequences. He's a 'typical' man. By the time we get to line 983 he's learnt his lesson, because he's been told to find out what women most desire, and he can't do it. He's not used to being subservient (which he has to be to the queen), he's not used to not getting his own way and he's not used to not having all the answers. It's no surprise that he's depressed. 'withinne his brest ful sorweful was the goost.'

In some ways he's changed from being an old-fashioned alpha male to being a more modern man, having to listen to women and pay attention. You might say he's getting in touch with his feminine side. Chaucer makes that clear with the image of the 24 ladies dancing, and then he meets the old crone, who's really horrible: 'A fouler wight ther may no man devise.' She's the one who'll tell him the answer he needs, but she exacts a heavy price for it as she insists that he does whatever she wants. That's a complete contrast from the beginning of the tale, when it was the knight who could do whatever he wanted. Chaucer's teaching us a lesson, that we can't always do what we want and we have to listen to others, particularly when they're members of the other sex. He's saying we don't have the rights we may imagine.

Examiner's commentary

- ◣ This has the potential to be a reasonable answer, because the student shows understanding of the transformation that the knight undergoes.
- ◣ The essay extract clearly deals with 'masculine roles', but would be improved by direct reference back to the terms of the question.
- ◣ There is straightforward comparison of the knight at the beginning of the tale and the knight later on.
- ◣ The expression is clear but too informal ('doesn't give a fig') and too repetitive. Concision is vital in an examination essay.
- ◣ There is the basis for a nuanced understanding of the knight's situation, but it fails because the student uses 'trendy' phrases – like 'alpha male' and 'feminine side' – without analysing them.
- ◣ Quotation is used, but is not integrated into sentences.
- ◣ There is an attempt to show how Chaucer the author creates meaning, but the significance of the image of the dancing ladies is merely mentioned rather than explained.

> ◥ Crucially, a better passage could have been chosen. Lines 1219–35 would have allowed direct discussion of the key concept of 'maistrie'.

If the rest of his examination answer reached this level of performance, it is likely this student would be on course to achieve a notional grade C.

Analysis in non-examined assessments

Student I

This student is undertaking the following task as a comparative non-examined assessment unit:

'Texts only work well if the reader can identify herself or himself with the situations, the people, the personal dilemmas that are presented in them. To want to read more, the reader has to feel personally involved.'

Comment on and analyse the connections and comparisons between *The Wife of Bath's Prologue* and *Tale* and Yann Martel's *Life of Pi* in the light of this comment.

Most strikingly, the Wife of Bath is not a person. She is a literary construct, created by Chaucer to serve a particular purpose, and she neither has nor should be expected to possess coherence of character. This discontinuity is easy to exemplify, because the licentiousness of a character who can revel in being 'refresshed half so ofte' as King Solomon is not the same as the sophisticated moralising represented in the tale's digression on gentillesse: 'looke who that is moost virtuous always.' Chaucer's original audience would have had no problem with this, because they were not expecting a psychologically consistent character. The modern reader may simply assign a consistency to her and so become 'personally involved', but that is a modern construct, not a medieval one. Pi, interestingly, is not necessarily a 'person' either. In this case, it is not a feature of the period, but of the nature of the text, which is a fantasy. Fantasy writing frees the author from the need to confine himself to psychological verisimilitude. It also distances the reader somewhat, asking them to take a more objective view of the subject matter.

Despite this, both authors seek to engage their audience by using the distinctive trick of making their narrators speak about memories. Pi Patel says he has 'vivid memories' of childhood times at the swimming pool. Martel achieves the illusion of a real person reminiscing with a recognisable comment on the way we look at the past: 'The appearance of things changed, of course, depending on the weather, the time of day, the time of year. But it's all very clear in my memory, as if it never changed.' Similarly the Wife is amused 'whan that it remembreth me upon my yowthe'. And similarly her vision is partial: she remembers herself only as unchangingly 'faire, and riche, and yong, and wel bigon'. This identical technique used by the two writers allows the reader to identify with the 'person' looking back through their lives, because this is something we all do. In this way the apparent former lives of the characters are established, so that they can be contrasted with their current circumstances and engage the reader with their stories, because they appear to be real people.

Examiner's commentary

This student:

▼ writes confidently with what is clearly a personal point of view – note the use of the word 'interestingly'

▼ makes very good references to the different ways in which texts have been written and can be received – she distinguishes very clearly between medieval and modern audiences and their likely responses

▼ uses phrases such as 'may simply assign' and 'not necessarily' to flag up the idea of multiple interpretations of text

▼ demonstrates clear attention to all five AOs even within this short extract

▼ interweaves *The Wife of Bath's Prologue* and *Tale* and *Life of Pi* within the same paragraph rather than treating them separately, using the language of connection in 'both authors seek' and 'while' to signal that she has found patterns of both similarity and difference between the texts

▼ writes very concisely, recognising that, in order to cover everything within the confines of a tight non-examination assessment word limit, she needs to write 'a lot about a little' not 'a little about a lot'.

If the rest of her NEA answer reached this level of performance, it is likely she would be on course to achieve a notional grade A.

Extended commentaries

In every kind of essay you will need to demonstrate your ability to analyse the way in which authors use language and form to create and shape meaning. You should practise this by writing analyses of particular passages from the text. This will have the added benefit of encouraging you to explore the text further, and will generate ideas that you can utilise in any essay you need to write.

Examples of such analyses are given below.

Commentary 1: lines 857–98

In seeming contrast to her naturalistic prologue, the Wife of Bath begins her tale with the conventional once-upon-a-time ('In th'olde dayes of the King Arthour') formula of a fairy tale, and indeed the tale will feature the supernatural elements of many a folk story. She also deliberately places the tale in the court of King Arthur, the legendary figure who even in the Middle Ages occupied a shadowy 'past' era of brave knights and honourable deeds. A large number of medieval tales were either written about or assimilated into the Arthurian tradition, so the audience might momentarily be lulled into thinking that the Wife is going to deliver a stock knightly romance, perhaps in the manner of *The Knight's Tale* of Palamon and Arcite. The first five lines of the tale seem to confirm this, with their talk of 'a land fulfild of faierie', and the elf-queen dancing in company – an image of harmony.

Chaucer's purpose, however, is very different. He permits the Wife to subvert the fairy tale genre rapidly and comprehensively. The irony begins subtly in lines 865–66, with the claim that the elves have been replaced by the 'limitours' and 'freres' with their 'grete charitee and prayeres'. It would seem that ancient superstition has been replaced by modern rational religion. The illusion is brief: in lines 878–81 Chaucer allows the Wife a savage attack on the Church, saying that the friar is an incubus who will dishonour women. For the attentive reader there is a clear echo of the phallic symbolism used in the description of the womanising Friar in *The General Prologue*, who was described as a 'noble post'.

The tale proper begins in line 882, and although the setting reverts to the 'honourable' past of King Arthur's time, the reader has been prepared for the inversions of expectation that are crucial to Chaucer's purpose. Instead of dancing and harmony, Chaucer provides the unexpected behaviour of the protagonist. The knight that 'king Arthour hadde in his hous' should be emblematic of knightly and Christian virtues, and normally we would expect to be introduced to his character and his qualities. Instead, at the very first moment and rather than protecting the maiden that he meets, 'by verray force, he rafte hire maidenheed.' The fairy tale form of the narrative is in direct conflict with its content and language, and Chaucer allows the Wife to utilise this to make her anti-male point. The nameless knight – itself almost a contradiction in Arthurian tales – is guilty of the worst possible crime against a woman, and is 'dampned … to be deed' because of it. The parallel with the 'incubus' friar is clear and deliberate. The whole tale will – like *The Wife of Bath's Prologue* – put men in the wrong. In a further subversion of the genre, Chaucer twists the form again by placing the knight's fate entirely in female hands, with the queen 'to chese wheither she wolde him save or spille'. The language is stark and uncompromising, and the audience is left in no doubt as to how it is supposed to view the knight's behaviour.

Commentary 2: lines 14–210

The interruption of the Wife at this stage of her prologue is significant, both structurally and artistically. In structural terms the two brief interruptions by the Pardoner in lines 163–68 and lines 184–87 signify the division between the Wife's opening 'theoretical' comments on marriage (lines 1–162), and her 'practical' experience with her husbands. Chaucer achieves this by naturalistic means, reminding the audience that they are notionally listening to the interplay of characters on the pilgrimage. The Wife's prologue is not a discourse or a soliloquy, it's the boasting talk of a woman who is trying to entertain and impress her fellow travellers. We do not forget either that she is a widow and would 'welcome the sixte' husband if she can catch one. This may well be one of the reasons she is on the pilgrimage in the first place, as there may be eligible bachelors riding alongside her. In this context Chaucer's choice of the Pardoner as the pilgrim who interrupts her is wildly comic. It is hinted in *The General Prologue* both that he is homosexually interested in the Summoner and that he is a eunuch. He is hardly the figure the Wife is hoping to impress.

Following this interruption the Wife begins to describe her marital experiences, and in this passage all Chaucer's virtues as a writer are visible. There is the colloquial verisimilitude of the Wife's speech patterns and references: 'as evere moote I drinken wyn or ale', 'as helpe me God'. There is her sarcastic and comic contempt for the manhood of her husbands – 'unnethe mighte they the statut holde' – broadening to the bawdy comedy of her own sexuality when she 'pitously a-night … made hem swinke'. Underlying it all is the thematic importance of what she is saying. She is boasting of her own dominance, that once she has married them she 'neded nat do lenger diligence to winne hir love'; Chaucer wants his audience to measure this attitude against Christian morality and expectations. A modern reader might miss the full shock of her denial of wifely obedience, but we can still laugh at the crudely calculating quality of her behaviour. She dominates her husbands both physically and mentally; they have 'yeven hir lond and hir tresoor'.

It is fruitful to consider alternative responses here. A medieval audience might see her simply as the embodiment of all that is worst about women – seeing her as covetous, disobedient, coarse and ignorant. They might have that response even while hugely enjoying her gusto and directness: 'and, by my fey, I tolde of it no stoor'. A modern reader, on the other hand, might view her as a forthright and admirable woman, challenging male authority and proclaiming a woman's right

Context

For a modern reader, the contexts are of absolute importance. You must constantly bear in mind the patriarchal nature of society in the fourteenth century, and view the Wife in relation to the subservient place of women at the time. Equally, you can hardly avoid reacting to passages like this with a modern sensibility. This is an ideal opportunity to address AOs 3 and 5.

to direct her own life. They might agree that she is a 'wys womman'. Both these types of response ultimately take a serious view of Chaucer's work as a whole, and that is probably right. It is perfectly possible, however, to view the whole of *The Canterbury Tales*, and particularly texts like *The Wife of Bath's Prologue* and *Tale*, as being 'purely' entertaining and as comedy for the sake of comedy. Such a view is legitimised here in the Wife's own comment, 'myn entente is nat but for to pleye' (line 192).

Commentary 3: lines 1219–64

Form, structure and language all come together in this tour de force at the end of *The Wife of Bath's Tale*. In form it is the necessary culmination of the fairy tale. The knight is faced with a final and crucial test, comparable to Gawain's temptation to preserve his life at the expense of his honour in *Sir Gawain and the Green Knight*. In the present case Chaucer modifies the traditional question to make the choice cruel, and relevant to the theme of obedience – the hag offers to be 'trewe, humble' but 'foul and old', or to be 'yong and fair', in which case he will have to 'take … aventure of the repair' that will happen. His decision to 'put me in youre wise governance' is not only formally unavoidable, but thematically central.

The structure of this passage exactly mirrors the end of the Wife's prologue, and the outcome is the same, with absolute dominance for the woman. Crucially, the language and vocabulary are identical, and feature the key terms of the Wife's discourse. 'Thanne have I gete of yow maistrie' here is identical to the 'I hadde geten unto me, by maistrie' of the prologue. 'Governance' and 'honour' are similarly paralleled, as is the outcome that the woman will only be 'trewe' to her husband once he has ceded absolute control to her. It is only in these circumstances that harmony can be achieved. 'Kis me,' the wife says when all her conditions have been fulfilled, and the fairy-tale quality of the opening of the tale, where the elf-queen 'daunced' 'with hir joly compaignie', is at last restored. With such a resolution the wife can afford to be magnanimous, she can become young and beautiful, and 'she obeyed him in every thing / That mighte doon him pleasance or liking'.

The tone seems set for the conventional ending: 'they lived happily ever after'. But this is Chaucer, and there is a final twist. The Wife of Bath cannot quite leave it at this; her prologue and tale must conclude as it began, with her viewpoint rather than that of tradition. Her desire for 'housbondes meeke, yonge, and fressh abedde' is entirely in keeping with her character but might be shared by many; her wish to 'overbide hem that we wedde' is a more sinister and entirely personal view. It is this narrative arc from the 'experience' of line 1 of her prologue to the 'pestilence' of line 1264 of her tale that gives *The Wife of Bath's Prologue* and *Tale* its extraordinary unity and makes it one of the greatest of Chaucer's achievements.

Top ten quotations

Before studying this section, you should identify your own 'top ten' quotations. Choose those phrases or sentences that seem to capture a key theme or aspect of the text most aptly and memorably, and clearly identify what it is about your choices that makes each one so significant. No two people studying *The Wife of Bath's Prologue* and *Tale* will select exactly the same set, and it will be well worth comparing and defending your choices with the other students in your class.

When you have done this, look carefully at the following list of quotations and consider each one's possible significance within the text. Discuss the ways in which each might be used in an essay response to support your exploration of various elements of *The Wife of Bath's Prologue* and *Tale*. Consider what these quotations tell us about Chaucer's ideas, themes and methods, as well as how far they may contribute to various potential ways of interpreting the text.

Experience, though noon auctoritee
Were in this world, is right ynogh for me
To speke of wo that is in marriage
(lines 1–3)

1

> The opening statement of the Wife of Bath's prologue is at the core of the whole text. In it, Chaucer makes the Wife a rebel, challenging the accepted conventions and expectations of her period and of her sex. We should not believe that these are Chaucer's own views; he places them in the Wife's mouth in order to form part of a wider argument about issues that run through *The Canterbury Tales* – morality, correct behaviour, marriage and attitudes to authority. The character he establishes is bold, assertive and uncompromising.

An housbonde I wol have, I wol nat lette,
Which shal be bothe my dettour and my thral
(lines 154–55)

2

> This is a bald statement of the Wife's belief in female dominance. There is no question of equality between the sexes, although even that would have been radical in the Middle Ages. The Wife states the extreme position, in keeping with the nature of her character and the purpose for which Chaucer has created her.

3

Deceite, weping, spinning God hath yive
To wommen kindely, whil that they may live.
(lines 401–02)

> This is a subtle moment in the prologue. The Wife takes an anti-feminist proverb and quotes it approvingly. The audience's response should be complex. They should detect the unfairness of the original (male) assertion, but they should also note the irony in the Wife boasting of a quality like deceitfulness that most people of either sex would condemn.

4

For trusteth wel, it is an impossible
That any clerk wol speke good of wives,
But if it be of hooly seintes lives
(lines 688–90)

> The Wife refers to the anti-feminist nature of all religious literature apart from the lives of saints (one of the most popular topics for medieval writers). She is pointing to a central feature of medieval Catholicism, whereby women were universally condemned because they shared Eve's guilt in leading Adam into Original Sin. At the same time, the medieval Church revered Mary, the mother of Christ, for her purity, and all saints for the same reason, so there was an ambivalence in attitudes to women that the Wife is quick to note.

5

And whan that I hadde geten unto me,
By maistrie, al the soverainetee
(lines 817–18)

> She uses the key words 'maistrie' and 'soverainetee' to describe the power she attains over her fifth husband, Jankin. It is the logical culmination of the intention she expressed in lines 154–55 and is at the centre of all she intends to express through her prologue and her tale.

6

He saugh a maide walkinge him biforn,
Of which maide anon, maugree hir heed,
By verray force, he rafte hire maidenhed
(lines 886–88)

> The abruptness and nature of the knight's crime are central to the Wife's purpose in telling the story. The whole of the prologue and tale are about the struggle for 'maistrie'. The knight expresses the extreme form of male mastery through rape; it is the Wife's intention to show the process by which he is humiliated and humbled, so that he can find happiness only once he has ceded absolute control to a woman.

Wommen desiren to have sovereinetee
As wel over hir housbond as hir love,
And for to been in maistrie him above.
(lines 1038–40)

7

> This is the Wife's central theme in both her prologue and tale, and repeats the key terms 'sovereinetee' and 'maistrie' from lines 817–18. Chaucer thus achieves both a structural and a thematic parallel in the prologue and tale, which is aesthetically satisfying and critical in reinforcing the Wife's views.

For gentillesse cometh fro God allone.
(line 1162)

8

> This is the only place in *The Wife of Bath's Prologue* and *Tale* where there is an insistence on the importance of virtue and the recognition that it is God-given. It is an important quotation, both in placing the Wife's beliefs in context and in showing how Chaucer is willing to step outside her characterisation in order to make the point. The Wife of Bath herself would avoid this kind of thinking and would not naturally allow it to intrude on her tale.

I put me in youre wise governance
(line 1231)

9

> This culmination of the tale is, to the Wife, a final example and vindication of her views. The couple can be happy only when the woman has total dominance over her husband. The inclusion of the word 'wise' is neat, and provokes the audience into considering and perhaps arguing over how far it is apt.

And eek I praye Jhesu shorte hir lives
That wol nat be governed by hir wives
(lines 1261–62)

10

> This is a beautifully judged finale. It is doubtless heartfelt from the Wife, but Chaucer invites us to explore the potential blasphemy of such a prayer. It is exactly in keeping with her opening assertion in lines 1–3, and forms an equal challenge to the patriarchal stance of the medieval Church, but the audience is left considering who may suffer most from the 'wo that is in mariage'.

Chaucer's work

Standard edition: *The Riverside Chaucer* (general editor Larry D. Benson, Oxford University Press, 3rd edn, 2008).

Modernised versions: strictly speaking, it is wrong to use the word 'translation' for Chaucer, as his work (like Shakespeare's) is written in English, albeit Middle English.

It is a very good idea to read some or all of the other *Canterbury Tales* in order to place *The Wife of Bath's Prologue* and *Tale* in its immediate context. There is a well-known verse rendering by Nevill Coghill (Penguin) and a prose 'retelling' by Peter Ackroyd (Penguin); the former attempts to give a flavour of Chaucer's verse, the latter is pacey and accessible. While these give a taste of Chaucer for the non-specialist, David Wright's *The Canterbury Tales: A Prose Version in Modern English* (Vintage) is better because it sticks closely to the original text and allows direct comparison with it. Although not currently in print it can easily be acquired second-hand. It omits the *Tale of Melibee* and *The Parson's Tale*, but is otherwise the best way to read the complete *Tales*.

Readings: the easiest way to hear Chaucer's work read aloud is via the internet; there are a number of sites that offer extracts or complete tales, and some give pronunciation guides too. See the section on internet resources below. Libraries may have audio CD versions.

Background reading

There is a daunting number of books and articles available on Chaucer. It is worth seeking out the following:

- Astell, A.W. (1996) *Chaucer and the Universe of Learning*, Cornell University Press. This places Chaucer in the context of his own learning and shows how that is reflected in his work.
- Beidler, P.G. (1996) *The Wife of Bath, Case Studies in Contemporary Criticism*, Bedford/St Martin's. This is invaluable as a guide to the most important approaches to *The Wife of Bath* – Marxist, feminist, etc.
- Bisson, L.M. (1999) *Chaucer and the Late Medieval World*, Macmillan. A good source of material on religion, class, commerce and sexuality.
- Brewer, D. (1996) *Chaucer and His World*, Eyre Methuen. This is an excellent visual and biographical account of Chaucer. Derek Brewer has written and edited a number of accessible books on Chaucer.
- Burrow, J. (1982) *Medieval Writers and Their Work: Middle English Literature and its Background 1100–1500*, Oxford University Press. This study places Chaucer in his literary context.

◥ Gray, D. (ed.) (2003) *The Oxford Companion to Chaucer*, Oxford University Press. This major volume amounts to a complete encyclopaedia of Chaucer and contains over 2000 entries.

◥ Hansen, E.T. (1992) *Chaucer and the Fictions of Gender*, University of California Press. This is very informative on medieval understandings of gender; Chapter 2 focuses on the Wife of Bath.

◥ Laskaya, A. (1995) *Chaucer's Approach to Gender in The Canterbury Tales*, D.S. Brewer. This is a very clear and worthwhile discussion, insisting on the need to consider multiple interpretations of texts; Chapter 9 deals specifically with *The Wife of Bath*.

◥ Leicester, H.M (1990) *The Disenchanted Self: Representing the Subject in The Canterbury Tales*, University of California Press. This focuses on Chaucer's craft and the voice created by each tale.

◥ Martin, P. (1990) *Chaucer's Women: Nuns, Wives, and Amazons*, University of Iowa Press. The author argues that women and relationships between the sexes are Chaucer's favourite subject, and that these relationships are a problem area.

◥ Nuttall, J. (2013) 'Voice and presence in *The Canterbury Tales*', *English Review* 23:4. The author explores how Chaucer creates and uses the voice of the narrator in the prologues to *The Pardoner's Tale* and *The Wife of Bath's Tale*.

◥ Patterson, L. (1991) *Chaucer and the Subject of History*, Routledge. This contains a very good reading of *The Wife of Bath's Prologue* and *Tale*, concentrating on history and subjectivity.

◥ Robertson, D.W. Jr (1962) *A Preface to Chaucer*, Princeton University Press. A difficult but important contribution to Chaucer studies.

◥ Rowland, B. (ed.) (1979) *Companion to Chaucer Studies*, Oxford University Press. An excellent collection of essays on the social and literary contexts for Chaucer's work.

◥ Shoaf, R.A. (1983) *Dante, Chaucer and the Currency of the Word*, Pilgrim. This has a chapter on *The Wife of Bath* and concentrates on the significance of economics, private wealth and individuality.

Online resources

The internet is a marvellous source of material on Chaucer, because it permits the use of illustrations and sound in a way that not even the best books can match. There is an enormous quantity of up-to-date material available, ranging from student guides to academic studies. A good search engine and the willingness to spend some time exploring will reveal considerable riches, and often unexpected and useful insights into all aspects of Chaucer's works, period and culture. The following sites are excellent starting points, but bear in mind that links and sites are liable to change.

www.unc.edu/depts/chaucer – the Chaucer Metapage; this should be your first port of call. It is designed to act as a guide to Chaucer resources on the internet and is frequently updated, so needs exploring.

http://afdtk.uaa.alaska.edu/pedagogy.htm – another good general site to start at.

www.kankedort.net – contains the Electronic Canterbury Tales and a wealth of other information.

http://sites.fas.harvard.edu/~chaucer/index.html – includes an interactive guide to Chaucer's pronunciation, grammar and vocabulary, and interlinear modernisations of some of the tales.

www.gutenberg.org/wiki/Main_Page – the homepage of Project Gutenberg, which exists to provide the texts of copyright-free material from all eras.

http://d.lib.rochester.edu/teams – the homepage of the Consortium for the Teaching of the Middle Ages; has introductions to, and the texts of, hundreds of medieval works.

http://legacy.fordham.edu/halsall/sbook.asp – the home of the Internet Medieval Sourcebook, a huge resource of medieval sources and texts, including information on pilgrimages, saints and relics.

www.sfsu.edu/~medieval/Volume5/Baumgardner.html – contains Rachel Ann Baumgardner's essay 'I Alisoun, I Wife: Foucault's Three Egos and the Wife of Bath's Prologue'.

www.luminarium.org/medlit/chaucessays.htm – has links to a range of essays about *The Wife of Bath*.

Film versions

The BBC made a series of modern adaptations based on *The Canterbury Tales* in 2003, including *The Wife of Bath* starring Julie Walters.

A 1972 film by Pier Paolo Pasolini, *I Racconti di Canterbury*, loosely treats eight of the tales, including *The Wife of Bath's Tale*.